WITHDRAWN

Sweet!

CELEBRATIONS

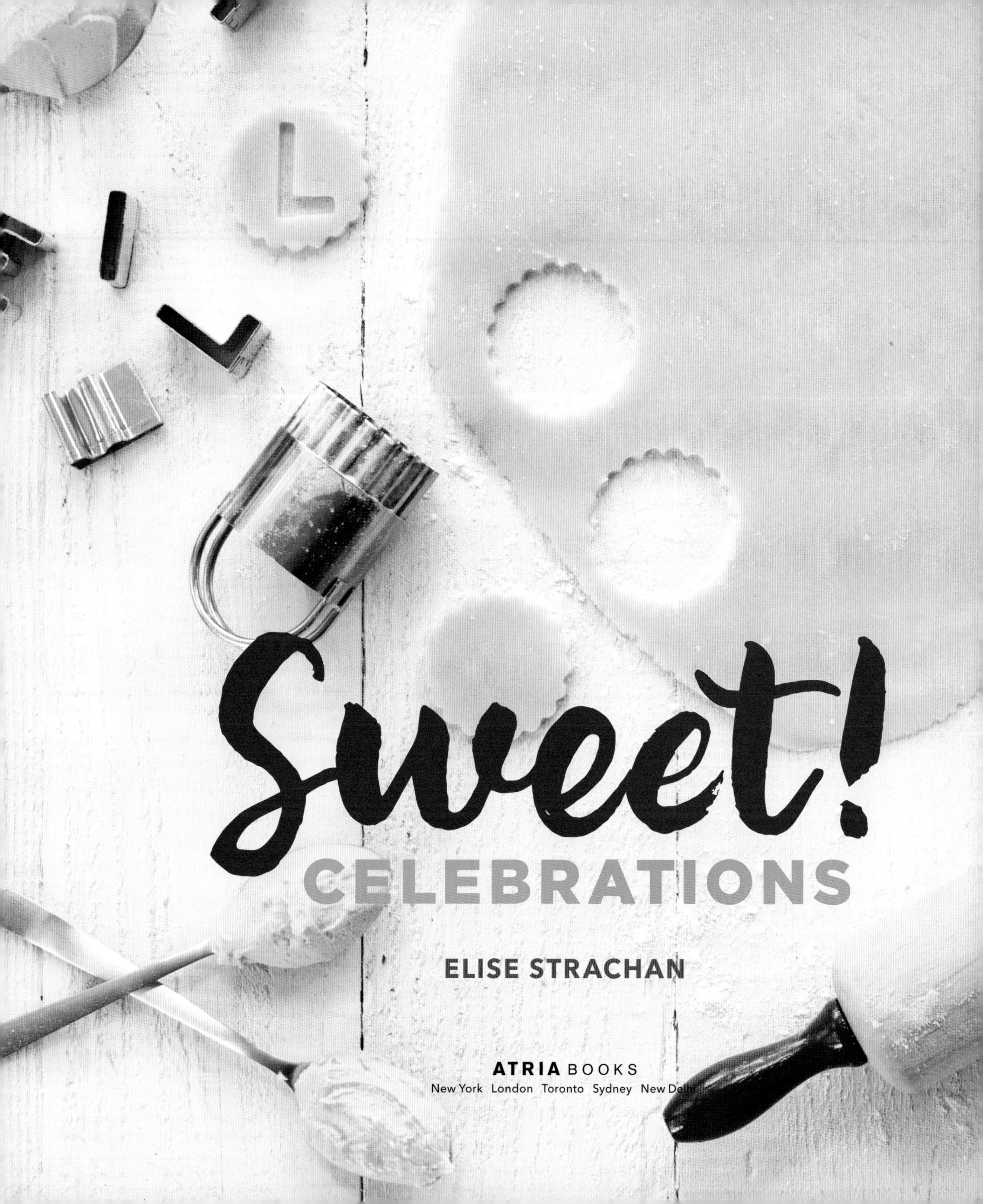

Sweet!
CELEBRATIONS

ELISE STRACHAN

ATRIA BOOKS

New York   London   Toronto   Sydney   New Delhi

ATRIA BOOKS

Atria Books
An Imprint of Simon & Schuster, Inc.
1230 Avenue of the Americas
New York, NY 10020

First Atria Books hardcover edition October 2016

ATRIA BOOKS and colophon are trademarks of Simon & Schuster, Inc.

For information about special discounts for bulk purchases, please contact Simon & Schuster Special Sales at 1-866-506-1949 or business@simonandschuster.com.

The Simon & Schuster Speakers Bureau can bring authors to your live event. For more information or to book an event, contact the Simon & Schuster Speakers Bureau at 1-866-248-3049 or visit our website at www.simonspeakers.com.

Photography by Lauren Bamford

Manufactured in China

10 9 8 7 6 5 4 3 2 1

Library of Congress Cataloging-in-Publication Data is available.

ISBN 978-1-5011-4222-2
ISBN 978-1-5011-4224-6 (ebook)

To MY PARENTS,
for never limiting my imagination.

To MY CHILDREN, for always
reminding me how much fun it is to
get messy in the kitchen.

And above all, to MY HUSBAND,
Alec, for being my rock, my support,
my best friend, and my biggest
advocate. Without you, none of this
would be possible.

CONTENTS

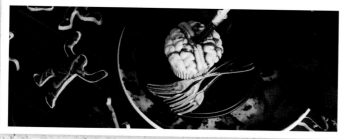

MEET ELISE

HI, I'M ELISE, a wife and mother of two boys who love to join me in the kitchen for baking, decorating, and making fun messes.

I've always loved baking, and as my creations got more adventurous, I decided to start posting dessert recipes online. I created My Cupcake Addiction—now on YouTube, Facebook, and Instagram—to share my love of amazing desserts with the world. There are millions of sweets enthusiasts following from every country imaginable, and requests for a cookbook have been pouring in, so I created this book for them, and for you!

The rising trend in dessert tables and party styling inspired me to create *Sweet! Celebrations,* a book that embraces every aspect of sweets entertaining. From the food and drinks to tips to style it up and a few DIY projects, this book has fun, creative, and simple ideas to suit any occasion.

Whether you're planning a Thanksgiving feast, a rustic wedding, an elegant high tea for friends, or the ultimate Halloween extravaganza, this beautiful book has it all. There are parties for the year's major holidays, from Valentine's Day to Christmas, as well as special occasions such as a spring garden party, colorful kids' party, and game-day desserts.

Whether you have twenty minutes to throw together a simple bake sale treat or all week to plan the ultimate party, you can pick and choose how big and crazy you want to get with your desserts from more than a hundred fun ideas.

This book has something for every skill level as well as fun tips for kids (like mine!) who love to help in the kitchen and ways to save time for those on the go.

Life is sweet, but it could always be a little bit sweeter!

Craft a **BACKDROP**

HOW TO USE THIS BOOK

Choose a **BIG CAKE**

Add some
CANDY

Decide on a
BEVERAGE

SWEET! CELEBRATIONS is a unique book and the first of its kind. It's a true entertainer's bible, with each chapter representing an occasion. Here you'll find ideas for those classic times throughout the year when entertaining is at its peak, as well as recipes for year-round treats, sweets, and bakes.

Every chapter begins with a themed large cake, the centerpiece of any party. I then follow this with three "small bake" recipes for each occasion—good for anyone who is asked to bring something small to a party. You'll find my tried and trusted basic recipes in the back of the book, on page 207, along with techniques, tips, and tricks for perfect cakes and bakes every time. And if you're not so keen on turning on the oven, there are two "no-bake" options included in each party chapter as well.

Tying the party together, I have two matching beverages to ensure your guests don't go thirsty. For fun crafting ideas, each chapter has two DIY elements as well as a few styling tips that help to accentuate your decor for entertaining.

Whether you want to throw an over-the-top party, surprise a friend, make a treat for the office, or organize a trick-or-treat to be remembered, you can pick and choose from recipes, ideas, and tips to sweetly style any occasion.

STYLE IT UP

"NO BAKE"
something fun

Pick a **SMALL BAKE** *or two*

WHAT'S IN MY PANTRY

FOR MOST RECIPES, you'll need to purchase at least some new ingredients, but as a rule I always keep my pantry stocked with the basics. And, of course, candy, which is essential.

I never toss leftover sprinkles, food coloring, or candy melts from a recipe. Instead I store them in jars to keep them fresh. I always save any unused candy items; you never know when you'll need a gummy bear or hard candy at short notice!

My pantry essentials are vanilla extract, flour, baking powder, sugar (granulated, superfine, brown, powdered, sanding), unsweetened cocoa, cinnamon, and nutmeg. My fridge always holds fresh eggs, milk, and butter for when the urge to bake strikes! I also like to have coconut oil on hand for thinning out my candy melts. And, of course, parchment paper and cupcake liners are a must in my house.

MY TOOLS OF THE TRADE

YOU DON'T NEED to buy every new baking tool on the market, but there are a few I love and use all the time. If you're looking to start your baking collection, begin with these multiuse basics.

1   Metal spatula
2   Offset spatula
3   Fat straws (or use wooden dowels)
4   Measuring cups
5   Piping bags and piping tips
6   Rubber/silicone spatulas
    (small and large)
7   Measuring spoons
8   Wooden spoon
9   Whisk
10 Graduated circle cutters
11 Cookie cutters
12 Metal ruler
13 Cake boards
14 Serrated knife
15 Grater or zester
16 Zip-seal plastic bags

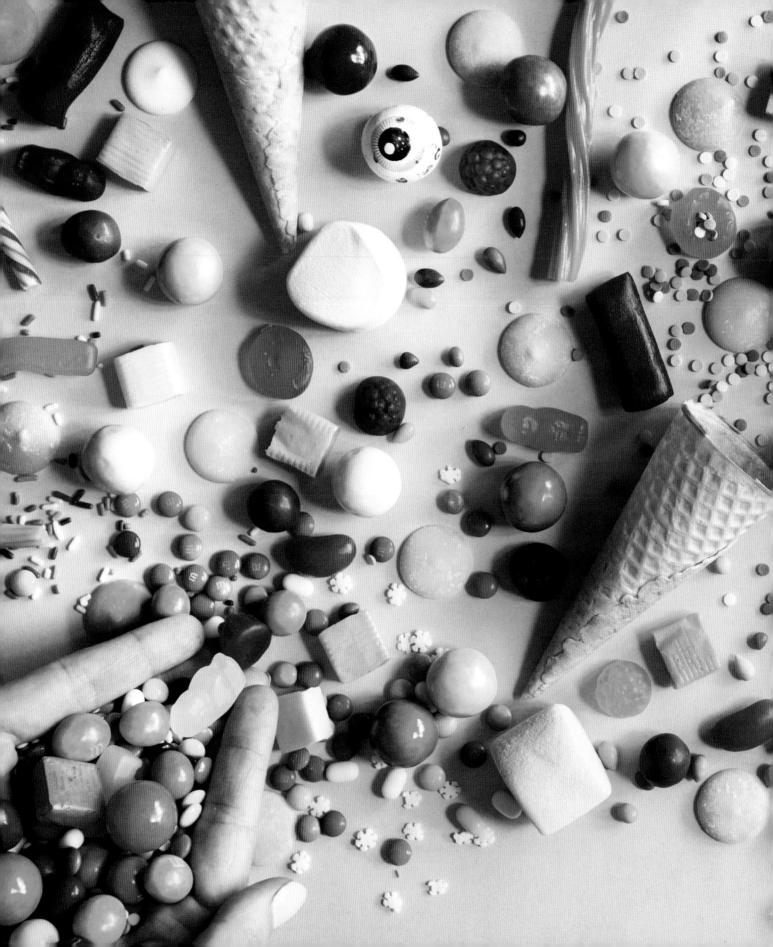

CANDY

WHEN IT COMES to candy, I try to put aside a small handful whenever I'm treating myself or the kids so I don't have to buy whole bags to re-create recipes. Store them in jars or plastic wrap, as you never know when you'll need three pink jelly beans to complete a dessert.

I love having an assortment of larger candy pieces like gumballs, marshmallows, and gummy snakes, as well as smaller pieces like novelty shaped sprinkles, jelly beans, and chocolate-coated sunflower seeds.

Variety is key when we're talking candy, and there's no such thing as too many options!

DECORATIVE STRAWS

FUN FINDS *you collect along the way:
mini pots, little baskets, and tiny
pompoms can add a lot to your desserts*

**ASSORTED
CAKE STANDS:**
*Make sure they vary in
height and color*

MASON JARS

MY STYLING ESSENTIALS

YOU DON'T NEED a huge selection to make a great party—a few key basics can go a long way.

CANDY JARS: *Three or four of these are plenty*

Mismatched **TEACUPS & SAUCERS**

11

LET'S
CELEBRATE

CONFETTI
LAYER CAKE

with pouring sprinkles illusion

MAKES ONE 4-LAYER CAKE

YOU'LL NEED

2 batches Classic Vanilla Cake
   batter (page 208)

¾ cup rainbow sprinkles

5 ounces white candy melts

10-inch cake board

Balloon stick with cup

2 batches Vanilla Bean
   Buttercream Frosting
   (page 215)

½ cup round confetti sprinkles

1 teaspoon light corn syrup

1. Preheat the oven to 350°F. Grease and flour two 8 x 3-inch round cake pans. Line the bottoms with rounds of parchment paper.

2. Make the cake batter and then very gently fold in the rainbow sprinkles. Do not overmix, as it will cause the sprinkle colors to run. Spoon the batter into the cake pans and bake until a wooden skewer inserted in the center of the cake comes out clean, 55 to 60 minutes. Check after 45 minutes, and if the top is browning too much, tent with foil.

3. Cool the cakes in the pans for 15 minutes, then run a metal spatula around the edge of the cakes and invert onto a wire rack to cool completely.

4. Melt the white candy melts (see page 220) and add a tablespoon to the center of the cake board. Place the cup for the balloon stick facedown on top of the melted candy and use a paintbrush to paint the remaining visible parts of the balloon stick cup with melted candy, leaving the small hole free and clear. Insert the balloon stick into the cup.

5. Carve and level the layers (see page 222, step 1), then slice each layer horizontally in half for a total of 4 layers.

6. Position the center of the first layer over the balloon stick and "thread" the cake down onto the board so that the stick pokes through the middle of the cake layer **A** . Continue to stack and layer (see page 222, step 2), threading the layers over the balloon stick as you go; the balloon stick should poke out of the center of the top layer.

7. Frost and smooth the cake (see page 223, step 4). Gently pat the confetti sprinkles around the bottom 1 inch of the cake to make a sprinkle border around the base **B** .

8. Paint the balloon stick with melted candy and pat confetti sprinkles onto the wet candy melts as you go, allowing excess sprinkles to fall haphazardly onto the top of the cake **C** .

9. Take an empty confetti sprinkles container and coat the inside with the corn syrup. Fill with sprinkles, pressing down to compact. Pour the sprinkles out, leaving a coating of sprinkles all around the inside.

10. Place a small blob of melted candy on the inside of one side of the container. Use the melted candy to "glue" the end of the balloon stick to the container, holding it in place until the melted candy has set and the container is glued in place **D** .

11. Add more confetti sprinkles to the top of the cake to give the illusion of a mound of freshly poured sprinkles.

IMPORTANT! *As the balloon stick is not edible, you* **MUST** *make sure that both the stick and the cup are removed as soon as the first slice of cake has been cut to avoid the possibility of choking.*

CONFETTI CUPCAKES

with hidden sprinkle surprise

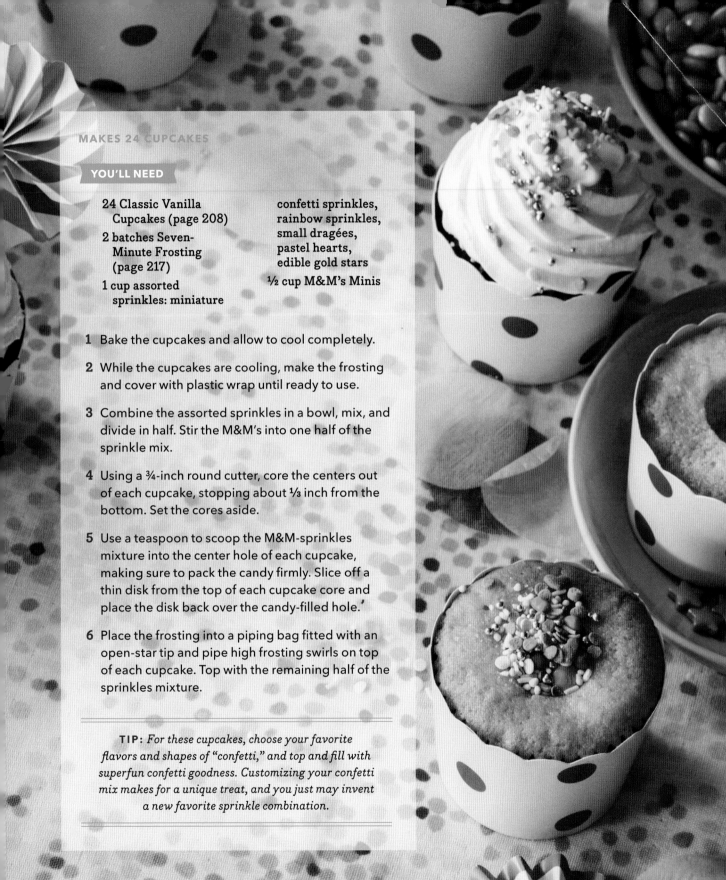

MAKES 24 CUPCAKES

YOU'LL NEED

24 Classic Vanilla
   Cupcakes (page 208)
2 batches Seven-
   Minute Frosting
   (page 217)
1 cup assorted
   sprinkles: miniature
confetti sprinkles,
rainbow sprinkles,
small dragées,
pastel hearts,
edible gold stars
½ cup M&M's Minis

1 Bake the cupcakes and allow to cool completely.

2 While the cupcakes are cooling, make the frosting
   and cover with plastic wrap until ready to use.

3 Combine the assorted sprinkles in a bowl, mix, and
   divide in half. Stir the M&M's into one half of the
   sprinkle mix.

4 Using a ¾-inch round cutter, core the centers out
   of each cupcake, stopping about ⅓ inch from the
   bottom. Set the cores aside.

5 Use a teaspoon to scoop the M&M-sprinkles
   mixture into the center hole of each cupcake,
   making sure to pack the candy firmly. Slice off a
   thin disk from the top of each cupcake core and
   place the disk back over the candy-filled hole.

6 Place the frosting into a piping bag fitted with an
   open-star tip and pipe high frosting swirls on top
   of each cupcake. Top with the remaining half of the
   sprinkles mixture.

TIP: *For these cupcakes, choose your favorite
flavors and shapes of "confetti," and top and fill with
superfun confetti goodness. Customizing your confetti
mix makes for a unique treat, and you just may invent
a new favorite sprinkle combination.*

BALLOON
CAKE POPS

MAKES 36 POPS

1 batch Chocolate Cake Pop Dough (page 212), chilled

5 ounces of each of 4 different colored candy melts

36 novelty curly straws

Styrofoam block

Mini confetti sprinkles

Pearl luster dust or shimmer powder

1 Line a plate or baking sheet with waxed paper. Roll the cake pop dough into a long sausage, about 1 inch in diameter. Using a knife, cut 1-inch lengths off the roll so you have even-size pieces. Roll each piece of dough into a firmly packed ball. Place the balls on the waxed-paper-lined plate or baking sheet and refrigerate 20 to 30 minutes to firm up.

2 Melt the candy melts (see page 220) to dipping consistency and place each color in a different bowl.

3 Dip the short end of a straw into some melted candy (whatever color you want the balloon to be) and insert the dipped end of the straw about ½ inch into the bottom of the cake pop ball.

4 While the candy seal is setting, gently taper the bottom of the cake ball into a point on the stick to create a traditional balloon shape.

5 Dip the cake pop into your desired melted candy color until the candy covers the entire balloon and a little of the straw. To make a confetti balloon pop, sprinkle confetti sprinkles onto the still-wet candy melts while turning the cake pop continuously to ensure even distribution.

6 Place the base of the straw into a piece of the Styrofoam block and allow the melted candy to completely set.

7 Using a toothpick, draw a small circle around the circumference of the straw where the melted candy meets the straw to form the balloon tie.

8 Once completely dry, use a paintbrush to brush with pearl luster dust to give a shiny transparent balloon effect.

TIME SAVER: *Cake pop dough can be frozen for up to a month and thawed at room temperature when required. It actually gets fudgier and more delicious with time in the freezer.*

COOKIE BUNTING FLAGS

MAKES ABOUT 32 FLAGS (5½ X 6 X 6 INCHES)

YOU'LL NEED

2 batches Vanilla Sugar Cookie dough (page 214)

Bunting Flag template (page 225)

All-purpose flour, for rolling out dough

1 fat straw or ¼-inch round cutter

5 ounces of each of 4 different colored candy melts

Mini confetti sprinkles

¼-inch ribbon

KIDS IN THE KITCHEN:
Let the kids get involved decorating the cookies for a unique and personal touch.

1. Make the cookie dough, divide into four portions, and chill for 30 minutes.

2. Trace the Bunting Flag onto a piece of thick paper and cut out to use as a template.

3. Preheat the oven to 350°F. Line a baking sheet with parchment paper.

4. Roll out a portion of the dough on a floured surface to a ¼-inch thickness.

5. With a sharp knife, use the template to cut flags from the rolled-out dough. Use a fat straw to make a ¼-inch round hole in the top two corners of each flag. Ensure that these are at least ¾ inch from any edge to avoid breakage when you string them up.

6. Place the cookies on the sheet and bake until the edges just start to turn golden brown, 10 to 12 minutes.

7. Let the cookies cool on the sheet for 5 minutes, then transfer them to a rack to cool completely. Repeat with the remaining dough portions.

8. Melt the candy melts (see page 220) to piping consistency.

9. Place the desired color melted candy into a zip-seal bag and cut a small tip off the corner.

10. Pipe a thin line of melted candy around the triangle, as well as the cut-out holes, close to the edge. You can make several outlines of the same color and allow them to dry.

11. Once the outline is dry, snip a larger corner from the zip-seal bag so you have a wider tip and "flood" the inside area of the cookie with melted candy. Tap the cookie gently to ensure even distribution and allow to set.

12. I made every third or fourth a confetti bunting flag, opting for plain white candy melts and sprinkling with confetti sprinkles before the melted candy has a chance to set.

13. Once all the flags are set, thread the ribbon through the cookie holes and tie a small knot at each hole, allowing your cookies to space out evenly as you go.

MINI COOKIE BIRTHDAY CAKES

MAKES 12 MINI "CAKES"

YOU'LL NEED

4 ounces white candy melts
24 vanilla sandwich cookies
12 birthday candles
Small round pink pearls or dragées
Rainbow sprinkles

1 Melt the candy melts (see page 220) to pouring consistency.

2 Take a sandwich cookie and place ½ teaspoon of melted candy on top. Place a second sandwich cookie on top to create a 4-layer cookie and allow to set.

3 Cut the top 1 inch off a candle and set aside along with 8 round pearls and some sprinkles. Take 1 teaspoon of melted candy and drop it in the middle of the top cookie. Tap on the work surface until the melted candy drizzles over the sides.

4 Add 8 pearls as "cherries" around the outside edge, place the candle in the center, and top with sprinkles. Repeat to make a total of 12 birthday cakes.

KIDS IN THE KITCHEN:
Get the kids to help stick the cookies together and decorate. This can get a little messy, but there's almost no preparation and loads of room for creativity.

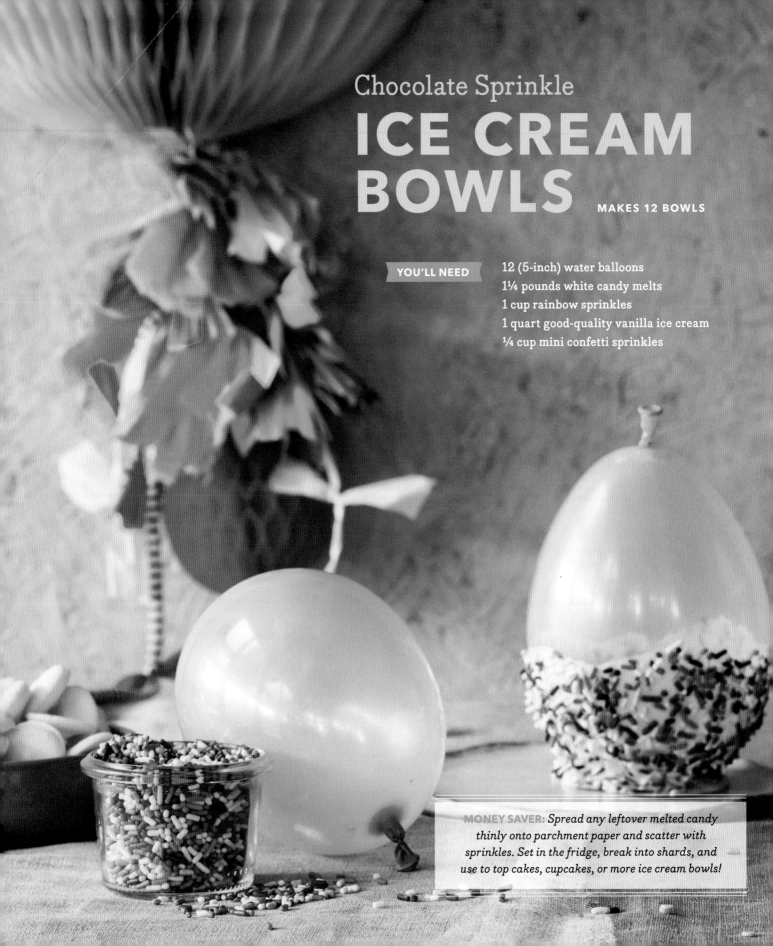

Chocolate Sprinkle
ICE CREAM BOWLS

MAKES 12 BOWLS

YOU'LL NEED

12 (5-inch) water balloons
1¼ pounds white candy melts
1 cup rainbow sprinkles
1 quart good-quality vanilla ice cream
¼ cup mini confetti sprinkles

MONEY SAVER: *Spread any leftover melted candy thinly onto parchment paper and scatter with sprinkles. Set in the fridge, break into shards, and use to top cakes, cupcakes, or more ice cream bowls!*

1 Inflate and tie the water balloons, wash, dry, and set aside.

2 Melt the candy melts (see page 220) to dipping consistency. *Make sure your melted candy is not hot.*

3 Dip a balloon into the melted candy until it comes one-third of the way up the sides of the balloon. Allow the excess to drip off and then hold the balloon over a piece of parchment paper before sprinkling with rainbow sprinkles, continually turning the balloon so the melted candy doesn't pool. Place the balloon standing up, not on its side, on a clean parchment-lined baking sheet.

4 Prepare 4 bowls and immediately place in the freezer to set before continuing to make all 12 bowls in sets of 4.

5 Once the balloon bowls have set, remove them from the freezer. Burst the balloon with a pin, toothpick, or skewer, removing any balloon membrane that may remain stuck to the melted candy.

6 To serve, fill each bowl with scoops of ice cream and top with 1 teaspoon of confetti sprinkles.

> **NOTE:** *While latex allergies are not very common, it pays to mention to your guests if you're using latex; or use latex-free balloons if you know someone with allergies is attending your event.*

ICE CREAM SODA FLOATS in ice cream cone cups

MAKES 12 SERVINGS

YOU'LL NEED

14 ounces white candy melts

12 flat-bottom ice cream cones

1½ cups vanilla ice cream

1½ cups soda of choice

6 cream-filled wafer cookies, halved on the diagonal

6 decorative straws

1 Melt the candy melts (see page 220) to pouring consistency.

2 Place 1 tablespoon of melted candy into each ice cream cone and turn to completely coat the inside of the cone, all the way to the rim.

3 Let set in the fridge and then repeat with an additional ½ tablespoon of melted candy. This makes your cone watertight. I always suggest a double coat to be safe.

4 Once the candy melt lining is set, use a small ice cream scoop to scoop vanilla ice cream into each cone. Pour in 2 tablespoons of soda, top with a cookie and straw, and serve immediately.

Cake Batter
MILKSHAKES

MAKES 6 SERVINGS

YOU'LL NEED

Rainbow sprinkles
6 standard milkshake glasses
6 cups whole milk
1 box (3.4 ounces) instant
  vanilla pudding mix
1 quart vanilla ice cream
1 cup heavy cream
6 maraschino cherries with
  stems
Decorative straws

1 Place ½ inch of water in a shallow dish and 1 inch of sprinkles in another.

2 Turn a milkshake glass upside down and dip in the water, then dip in the sprinkles to create a sprinkled rim around the edge of the glass.

3 In a blender, combine the milk, pudding mix, and ice cream and blend until smooth, thick, and creamy.

4 Using an electric mixer, whip the heavy cream to firm peaks and place in a piping bag fitted with a star tip.

5 Pour the milkshake into the glasses, stopping just below the line of sprinkles. Top with a swirl of whipped cream, additional sprinkles, a cherry, and a straw.

TIME SAVER: *I recommend rimming the glasses in advance. When ready to serve, blend the ingredients, pour, top, and sprinkle to ensure fresh, thick, ice-cold shakes.*

DIY № 1

CONFETTI
UTENSIL SETS

GLUE

YOU'LL NEED

Paper confetti sprinkles

Disposable utensils (I love the wooden ones)

Craft glue (nontoxic)

Ribbon

GET CRAFTY

1. Place all the confetti in a tall cup.

2. Coat the handles of your utensils thoroughly with craft glue.

3. Dip into the confetti and smooth with your hands.

4. Tie with ribbon to make sets.

TIP: *Use this technique to customize gift bags, invitations, and more, to theme your event.*

TIP: *Rubbing the finished balloons on clothing or fabric before hanging helps the confetti stick to the insides of the balloon.*

YOU'LL NEED

Small funnel

Transparent balloons

Paper confetti sprinkles

GET CRAFTY

1 After assembling your materials **A**, insert a small funnel into the neck of a balloon and pour in a handful of confetti **B**.

2 Inflate the balloon, tie, and vigorously shake before hanging **C**.

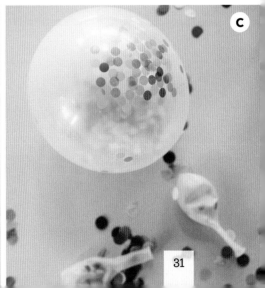

I love how versatile this party theme is. You can easily take this party from a brightly colored kids' party to a fun teens' event, and back to pastels for a beautiful baby shower. Whatever the reason, is there ever an occasion that's not made better with sprinkles?

LET'S CELEBRATE
PARTY

REMEMBER TO stick to your color palette throughout—brights, pastels, or neons. As long as you have one consistent theme running throughout, your party will flow beautifully.

For a simple backdrop, cut assorted sizes of rounds from colored craft paper and stick it to the wall: It looks just like giant sprinkles!

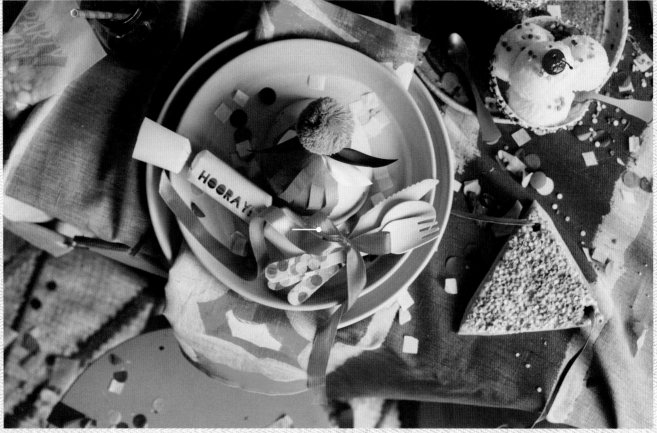

There's something just so fun about sprinkles, confetti, and bright colors. Throw in a nod to old-school soda shops, decadent ice cream treats, and a surprising illusion cake, and you've got all the elements to create a total "wow factor" party.

35

SWEETS
FOR MY SWEET

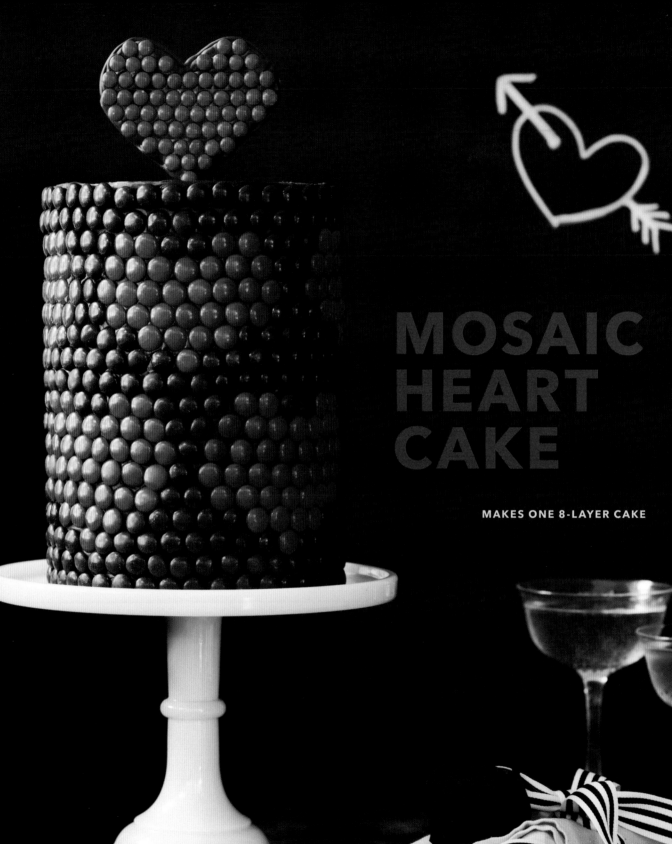

MOSAIC HEART CAKE

MAKES ONE 8-LAYER CAKE

2 batches Dark Chocolate
   Ganache (page 218)

2 batches Rich Chocolate Mud
   Cake batter (page 211)

8-inch cake board

5-inch thin cake board

Love Heart template (page 225)

3½ ounces chocolate candy
   melts

½ cup red M&M's Minis

About 1 pound brown M&M's

About 10 ounces red M&M's

1 Make the ganache and allow to cool at room temperature to spreading consistency.

2 Preheat the oven to 325°F. Grease and flour four 6 x 3-inch round cake pans. Line the bottoms with rounds of parchment paper. (If you only have two pans, do this in batches, and do not mix up the second batch of batter until you're ready to bake the second set of cakes.)

3 Make the cake batter, scrape into the pans, and bake until a wooden skewer inserted in the center of a cake comes out clean, about 1¼ hours.

4 Cool in the pans for 15 minutes, then run a metal spatula around the edge of the cakes and invert onto a wire rack to cool completely.

5 Carve and level the cakes (see page 222, step 1). Slice each cake horizontally into 2 even layers. Starting with the 8-inch cake board, stack and layer the cakes (see page 222, step 2). Add supports and the 5-inch cake board (see page 222, step 3) at the fourth layer. Frost and smooth the cake (see page 223, step 4).

6 Place a piece of parchment over the Love Heart template and trace 9 hearts. Cut around 8 of the hearts and leave one intact on the parchment and reserve for the topper.

TIP: If the chocolate starts to set too quickly, use a hair dryer on low to gently warm it up again.

7 Melt the candy melts (see page 220) and place in a zip-seal bag, cutting off a small corner to make a fine tip. Place a wooden skewer at the bottom point of the reserved template, positioning it about halfway up. Pipe the outline of the heart with the melted candy, making sure to go over the skewer A . Let the outline set.

8 Pipe thick lines of melted candy across the heart, affixing rows of red M&M's Minis until the whole heart is covered B .

9 Stick the 8 parchment hearts evenly around the outside of the cake—the ganache will hold these in place C . Start at the bottom of the cake and line up brown M&M's in even rows and ensure the "M" isn't showing. Any time you encounter a heart, peel back the paper and place red M&M's in its place, keeping the lines straight D . Feel free to add a little more ganache to the top of the cake before adding the final row.

10 Once set, remove the heart topper from the parchment, trim the skewer to size, and place it on top.

CHOCOLAT
MUG
BROWNIES
perfect for two

YOU'LL NEED

2 tablespoons granulated sugar

1 tablespoon light brown sugar (or just extra granulated if you have no brown)

2 tablespoons salted butter, melted

½ teaspoon vanilla, orange, peppermint, or coffee extract

1 large egg yolk

1 tablespoon olive oil

2 tablespoons water

¼ cup all-purpose flour

1 tablespoon unsweetened cocoa powder

¼ teaspoon baking powder

3 tablespoons semisweet chocolate chips

2 medium mugs

Ice cream and toppings, for serving

MAKES 2 SERVINGS

1 In a medium bowl, combine the sugars, butter, and vanilla and mix with a wooden spoon until smooth. Add the egg yolk, oil, and water and mix to combine.

2 Add the flour, cocoa, and baking powder and mix until there are no lumps. Fold in the chocolate chips.

3 Evenly spoon into 2 microwave-safe mugs. Microwave on high in 30-second intervals until the brownies spring back when touched in the center, about 1 minute.

4 Top with ice cream and your favorite toppings and serve piping hot.

Love Note

FORTUNE COOKIES

2 extra-large egg whites

½ teaspoon vanilla extract

½ cup sifted (60g) all-purpose flour

½ cup (95g) superfine sugar

18 handwritten love notes

2 ounces white candy melts

2 ounces pink candy melts

Red, pink, or white sprinkles

MAKES 18 COOKIES

YOU'LL NEED

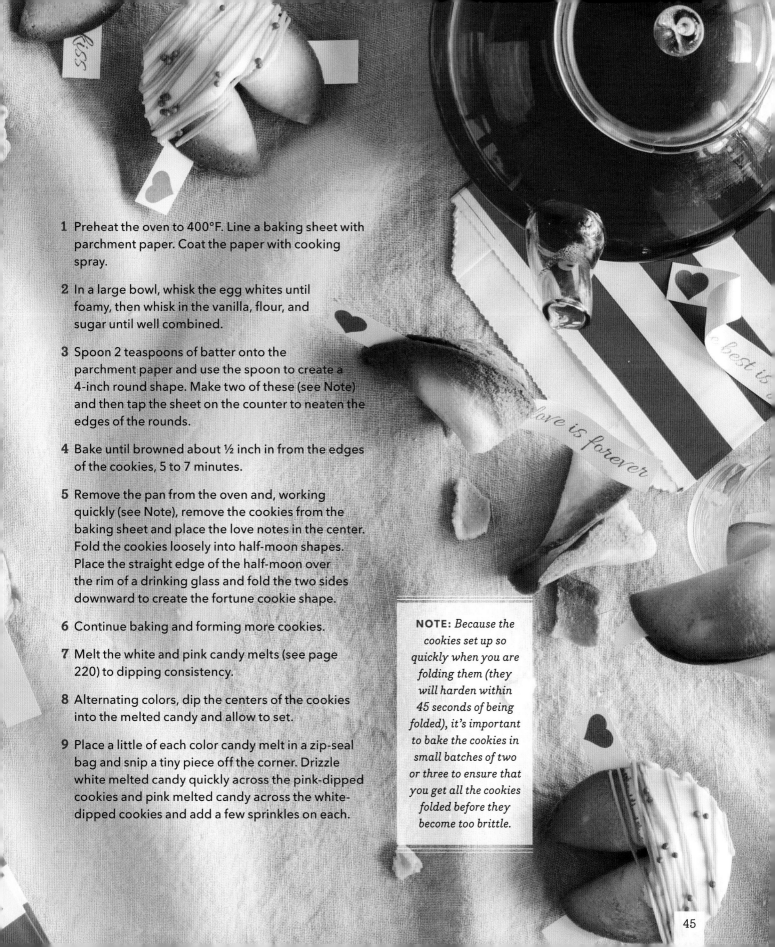

1 Preheat the oven to 400°F. Line a baking sheet with parchment paper. Coat the paper with cooking spray.

2 In a large bowl, whisk the egg whites until foamy, then whisk in the vanilla, flour, and sugar until well combined.

3 Spoon 2 teaspoons of batter onto the parchment paper and use the spoon to create a 4-inch round shape. Make two of these (see Note) and then tap the sheet on the counter to neaten the edges of the rounds.

4 Bake until browned about ½ inch in from the edges of the cookies, 5 to 7 minutes.

5 Remove the pan from the oven and, working quickly (see Note), remove the cookies from the baking sheet and place the love notes in the center. Fold the cookies loosely into half-moon shapes. Place the straight edge of the half-moon over the rim of a drinking glass and fold the two sides downward to create the fortune cookie shape.

6 Continue baking and forming more cookies.

7 Melt the white and pink candy melts (see page 220) to dipping consistency.

8 Alternating colors, dip the centers of the cookies into the melted candy and allow to set.

9 Place a little of each color candy melt in a zip-seal bag and snip a tiny piece off the corner. Drizzle white melted candy quickly across the pink-dipped cookies and pink melted candy across the white-dipped cookies and add a few sprinkles on each.

NOTE: Because the cookies set up so quickly when you are folding them (they will harden within 45 seconds of being folded), it's important to bake the cookies in small batches of two or three to ensure that you get all the cookies folded before they become too brittle.

1 batch Vanilla Sugar Cookie dough (page 214),
plus flour for rolling out

Red food coloring

4-inch heart cookie cutter

3-inch heart cookie cutter

2 cups Conversation heart candy

Mini pastel confetti sprinkles

Mini gold pearl sprinkles (dragées)

7 ounces different colored candy melts (I used pink and red)

Small candies or gifts

1   Make the cookie dough and tint it deep red. Divide the dough into two portions and chill for 30 minutes.

2   Preheat the oven to 350°F. Line a baking sheet with parchment paper.

3   On a floured surface, roll one portion of the dough to a ¼-inch thickness. Working in sets, use the 4-inch cookie cutter to cut 4 large hearts for each completed cookie box and place the cookies on the lined baking sheet.

4   Take the 3-inch cookie cutter and cut a smaller heart out of the center of 2 of the large hearts. Reroll the scraps and cut out more cookies.

5   Bake until you just start to see the cookies darkening around the edges, 10 to 12 minutes. Allow to cool slightly before removing from the baking sheet.

6   Repeat with the remaining portion of dough.

7   Place half of the conversation heart candy into a zip-seal bag and use a rolling pin to lightly crush them. Add the sprinkles and pearls and shake to combine.

8   Melt the candy melts (see page 220) to piping consistency.

9   Place the desired color candy melts into a zip-seal bag, cutting a small tip off the corner. Pipe a thin line of melted candy around the edge of one of the solid hearts. Then take a heart cookie with the center removed and place it on top. Pipe a line of melted candy on top and place another heart cookie with the center removed on top.

10 Fill the center of the gift box with whole conversation hearts, your favorite candy, or a small gift, and then pipe a line of melted candy on top of the hollow heart and place the final whole heart cookie on top.

CONVERSATION HEART PIÑATA COOKIES

edible gift boxes   MAKES 6 COOKIE "BOXES"

11. Pipe a thin line of melted candy around the top heart, close to the outside edge. Once the outline is dry, snip a larger corner from the zip-seal bag so you have a wider tip and "flood" the inside area of the cookie with melted candy. Tap the cookie on the counter to ensure even distribution and immediately sprinkle with the crushed candy mixture.

12. Place several whole conversation hearts among the crushed candy and allow to set.

13. Repeat to make all the boxes, changing the color of candy melts as you go.

KIDS IN THE KITCHEN:
Get the kids to stuff and join the piñata cookies— they'll love it!

TIME SAVER:
These cookies will last up to a week at room temperature, so feel free to make them in advance.

STRAWBERRY CHEESECAKE ICE POPS

MAKES 10 FROZEN POPS

YOU'LL NEED

4 cups coarsely chopped strawberries (2 pounds)
2 tablespoons granulated sugar
8 ounces cream cheese, at room temperature
½ cup powdered sugar
Pink food coloring (optional)
½ cup heavy cream
1 cup (3½ ounces) crushed shortbread cookies
2 tablespoons salted butter, melted
10 wooden pop sticks

Place the strawberries in a medium bowl and sprinkle with the granulated sugar. Allow to sit for 15 minutes at room temperature.

In a medium bowl, combine the cream cheese and powdered sugar and beat until very well combined. Pour the strawberries and any accumulated juices into the cream cheese mixture and gently fold in. For an enhanced "strawberry"-looking pop, add a little pink food coloring.

Fold in the heavy cream using large sweeping motions. Do not overbeat.

In a medium bowl, stir the shortbread crumbs and butter to combine. The mixture should resemble wet sand.

Spoon the cheesecake mixture into ten 3-ounce cavities of an ice pop mold, filling three-fourths full. Bang the mold on the counter to compact the mixture.

Spoon in the cookie crumb mixture and press down gently to compact, add the wooden pop sticks, and freeze for 6 hours (overnight is best).

Chocolate Raspberry
COOKIE POTS

MAKES 4 SERVINGS

YOU'LL NEED

½ cup crushed chocolate sandwich cookies (about 5, cream filling left in)

1 tablespoon salted butter, melted

4 (½-pint) wide-mouthed jelly jars

3½ ounces semisweet chocolate, chopped

1¼ cups heavy cream

1 container (6 ounces) raspberries

Fresh mint

1. In a bowl, stir the crushed cookies and butter to combine. The mixture should resemble wet sand.

2. Spoon 1 heaped tablespoon of the mixture into the bottom of each jar and press to compact.

3. Melt the chocolate and ¼ cup of the heavy cream together, stirring until smooth. Set aside to cool.

4. With an electric mixer, whip ¾ cup of the cream to very soft peaks. The cream should be just starting to look light and fluffy, but the beaters shouldn't be leaving a mark.

5. Fold in the chocolate mixture with a wooden spoon and big sweeping movements. Spoon the chocolate mousse into a piping bag and cut the end. Pipe ½ inch of mousse on top of the cookie base in each jar and tap on the counter to settle.

6. Set aside 4 nice-looking raspberries to use for garnish. Divide the remaining raspberries among the jars, placing them on top of the mousse, right against the side of the jar. Pipe in more mousse until the jar is filled. Using an offset spatula, smooth the top of the mousse so it's flush with the top of the jar.

7. Just before serving, use an electric mixer to whip the remaining ¼ cup heavy cream to stiff peaks and place a dollop on top of each pot, along with a raspberry and a sprig of mint.

"Spice It Up" CHILI HOT CHOCOLATE

MAKES 2 SERVINGS

YOU'LL NEED

3 cups whole milk

1 cinnamon stick

1 fresh cayenne or serrano chili, quartered

5 ounces semisweet chocolate, chopped

2 medium mugs

Whipped cream, for serving

1. In a medium saucepan, combine the milk, cinnamon stick, and chili and simmer for 15 minutes. Remove from the heat and set aside for 15 minutes (or longer for more of a kick) to infuse.

2. Strain out the chile and cinnamon stick and heat the milk mixture until it comes to a low boil. Remove from the heat and add the chocolate, stirring until the chocolate has completely melted.

3. Pour into the mugs, top with whipped cream, and serve immediately.

LOVE POTION #9

YOU'LL NEED

6 tablespoons grenadine
24 ice cubes
6 martini glasses
1 bottle (1.25 liters) lemon-lime soda
    (such as Sprite)
6 decorative straws
6 large strawberries

Place the grenadine and ice cubes in a blender and pulse to make red crushed ice. Spoon an equal amount into each glass, top with soda, add a straw, and garnish with a strawberry.

SWEET SURPRISE BON-BONS

YOU'LL NEED

- Red and pink tissue paper
- Cardboard tubes from paper towel rolls (or Pringles containers for larger gifts)
- Adhesive tape
- Colored ribbon
- Love notes and gifts
- Red and pink patterned craft paper

GET CRAFTY

1. Lay the tissue paper on a flat surface.
2. Place a cardboard tube in the center (cut to size for smaller or larger crackers).
3. Cover the roll with tissue paper, taping in the center.
4. Twist one end and secure with ribbon.
5. Stuff the cracker with love notes and gifts .
6. Twist the opposite end of the tissue paper and secure with ribbon.
7. Cut a rectangle of craft paper and wrap around the tube, leaving the tissue paper ends free. Secure with tape.

A romantic take on Christmas crackers, these sweet surprise bon-bons are designed to be filled with cheeky romantic notes for your loved one, favors for guests, or a romantic gift.

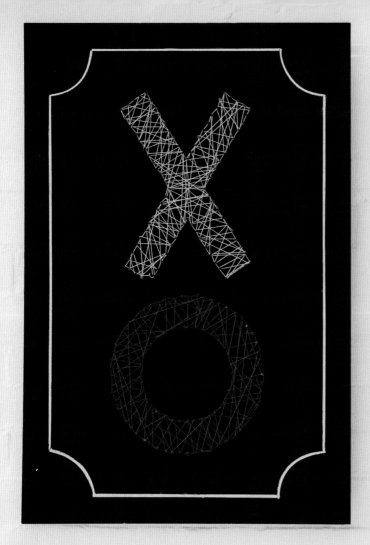

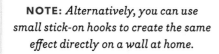

NOTE: *Alternatively, you can use small stick-on hooks to create the same effect directly on a wall at home.*

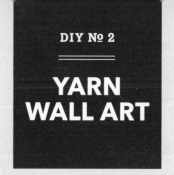

DIY № 2

YARN WALL ART

YOU'LL NEED

Chalkboard paint or your desired color of regular paint

Paint roller

1 large wooden art block

Craft paper

1 package ½-inch nails

Hammer

Red and pink heavy cotton embroidery thread or lightweight yarn

GET CRAFTY

1 If desired, paint your art block and allow to dry.

2 Map out your shape using craft paper and cut to create a template **A**.

3 Position your template on the painted board and secure in place with a couple of well-placed nails around the edges of the shape.

4 Hammer in a small nail every 1 inch all the way around the shape **B**. Remove the craft paper.

5 Take the thread and tie it off on a nail, then wind it from one side to the other, wrapping around a different nail each time to create a large cross-stitch-looking picture **C**.

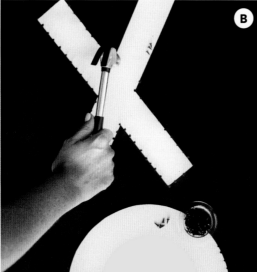

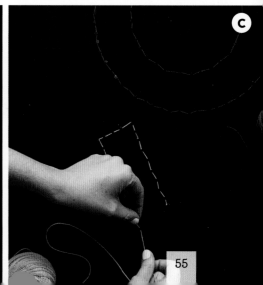

55

Valentine's Day aside, there are so many reasons to celebrate love! An engagement, a wedding, a vow renewal, a new baby on the way, or a new home to celebrate. What's not to love about love?

SWEETHEARTS
PARTY

WITH ALL that red, pink, and white, it's important to add a pop of pattern into the mix. I used bold striped ribbons on my place settings. You can get creative by covering boxes or stacks of books in patterned craft paper to add elevation to the table elements as well as a burst of bold color.

Rather than giving and receiving expensive Valentine's gifts, I prefer something from the heart. Homemade fortune cookies are so incredibly personal, and creating a night to remember is worth more than all the little blue boxes in the world. Well, almost . . .

I remember my dad buying Valentine's chocolates for my mother and she'd always share them with my brother, sister, and me. She said Valentine's was about celebrating all the people you love, not just one special person, so now that I have kids of my own, that tradition continues (much to their delight).

For a unique backdrop I used large chalkboard wall decals and hand-drew the Eiffel Tower to instantly transform my dining room into a romantic French restaurant.

SPRING FLING

"Naked"
FLOWER
CAKE

MAKES ONE 6-LAYER CAKE

1 Preheat the oven to 325°F. Grease and flour three 6 x 3-inch round cake pans. Line the bottoms with rounds of parchment paper. (If you only have two pans, do this in batches, and do not prepare the half batch of batter until you're ready to bake the third cake.)

2 Make the cake batter and divide among the cake pans. Bake until a skewer inserted into the center of each cake comes out clean, about 1 hour 10 minutes. Cool completely in the pans, then run a metal spatula around the edge of the cakes and invert the cakes onto a wire rack to cool completely.

3 Make the buttercream frosting.

4 While the cake is baking, make a simple syrup: In a saucepan, combine the water and sugar and heat until the sugar is completely dissolved. Set aside to cool.

5 Carve and level the cakes (see page 222, step 1). Slice each cake horizontally into two even layers, creating six layers in total. Brush all the layers with some simple syrup.

6 Place a little frosting onto the 8-inch cake board and lay a cake layer on top. Place some frosting into a piping bag fitted with a plain tip and pipe a 1-inch-diameter border around the rim of the layer. Fill inside the border of each layer with more frosting and level off with a spatula.

7 Top with three more cake layers, repeating the frosting in between, as well as on the fourth layer. Add four supports and the 5-inch cake board (see page 222, step 3). Place a tablespoon of frosting in the center of the cake board and continue stacking and frosting the remaining two cake layers **A**.

8 Using a metal ruler, gently scrape the sides of the cake, pushing the frosting into the layers and letting it smudge onto the sides of the cake layers a little **B**.

9 Wrap a length of textured ribbon around the bottom of the cake **C** and "glue" at the back with a little frosting.

10 Cut a small piece of floral foam and wrap in plastic wrap to protect the cake from touching the foam. Place the foam on the 4-inch cake board and stick seasonal flowers into the covered floral foam. Use a little frosting to secure the cake board with the flower arrangement to the top of the cake **D**.

> **TIME SAVER:** *Minus the flowers, this entire cake can be frozen fully made for up to 2 weeks.*

Vegetable
GARDEN POT CUPCAKES

MAKES 24 CUPCAKES

24 Classic Chocolate Cupcakes (page 209)
½ batch Milk Chocolate Ganache (page 219)
24 mini terra-cotta pots (about 3 inches)
1 cup crushed chocolate sandwich cookies
    (about 10, cream filling left in)
24 each orange and purple Starburst candies
18 red Starburst candies
Very small sprigs fresh mint

1 Bake the cupcakes as directed and let cool completely.

2 Make the ganache to pouring consistency.

3 Place each cooled cupcake into a mini terra-cotta pot, pushing it down to just below the pot rim, and spoon a little ganache over the top of each cupcake, ensuring it does not drip over the sides of the pots.

4 Sprinkle with crushed cookies to create "dirt."

5 Cut the orange Starburst candies in half. Roll each piece and taper the tip to resemble a small carrot.

6 Cut the purple Starburst candies in half. Roll each piece into a ball and taper the tip to resemble beets.

7 Cut each of the red Starburst candies into quarters. Roll each piece into a ball and taper at the bottom to form a radish.

8 Using a toothpick or skewer, poke a small hole in the top of each of the "vegetables" and insert a sprig of mint.

9 Divide the vegetables into groups of 2 carrots, 2 beets, and a small bunch of 3 radishes. Scrape back a little of the cookie "dirt" to reveal fresh ganache before sticking the vegetables onto the cupcakes.

BEEHIVE MERINGUES

on a chocolate honeycomb base

MAKES 12 BEEHIVES

YOU'LL NEED

4 extra-large egg whites, at room temperature

1 cup plus 2 tablespoons (220g) superfine sugar

2 teaspoons cornstarch, sifted

1 teaspoon distilled white vinegar

5 or 6 drops yellow food coloring

9 ounces yellow candy melts

12-inch square of clean, dry bubble wrap, with ½-inch "bubbles"

3-inch round metal cookie cutter

24 small yellow jellybeans

Black edible marker

48 sliced almonds

1 Preheat the oven to 215°F (these cook low and slow). Line a baking sheet with parchment paper.

2 Place the egg whites in a clean, dry bowl (I prefer metal or glass bowls when beating egg whites). Beat with an electric mixer on high speed until soft peaks form. Gradually add the sugar in thirds, beating well after each addition. Continue beating until the mixture is glossy and it ribbons from the end of the beater when lifted, then continue beating another 2 minutes.

3 Add the cornstarch, vinegar, and food coloring and beat until just combined.

4 **Make the beehives:** Place the mixture into a piping bag with a ¼-inch plain tip. In a continuous swirl, pipe a 2-inch-diameter base onto the baking sheet, and continue piping in a circle, lifting the piping tip as you go to create height, and making each swirl a little smaller as you go (to resemble a beehive). At the end, pull up the meringue to make a little peak. Pipe a total of 12 beehives.

5 Bake until the beehives are completely dry when tapped on the base and they come off the baking sheet with no resistance, about 2½ hours. Turn the oven off and leave the meringues in the cool oven to dry overnight.

6 **Make the honeycomb:** Melt the candy melts (see page 220). Set aside ½ cup for later. Let the remaining melted candy cool slightly, then spread it evenly across the sheet of bubble wrap using an offset spatula. Place on a tray in the fridge to set for 5 to 7 minutes. Once set, carefully peel away the bubble wrap to reveal the honeycomb.

7 Fill a shallow bowl with boiling water and place the cookie cutter into the water for about 30 seconds. Use the hot cookie cutter (caution!) to gently cut 12 rounds from the honeycomb.

8 **Make the bees:** Take a jellybean and draw on stripes and eyes using the marker. Use a little melted candy to affix a sliced almond to each side as wings.

9 Take a beehive and place 1 teaspoon of melted candy on the base, then affix it to the honeycomb. With a toothpick, place a small drop of melted candy onto the base of a bee and affix 2 or 3 bees to the sides of the beehives.

TIME SAVER: *Meringues can be made ahead and stored in an airtight container for up to 2 weeks.*

CARROT CAKE POPS

cookie dirt garden
MAKES 24 POPS

YOU'LL NEED

- ½ batch Chocolate Cake Pop Dough (page 212)
- 24 miniature waffle ice cream cones
- 10-inch wooden skewers
- 6 ounces orange candy melts
- Floral foam
- Fresh mint, cut into bushy sprigs
- 3 to 4 cups crushed chocolate sandwich cookies (15 to 20 cookies, cream filling left in)

1 Make the cake pop dough and press the mixture firmly into the waffle cones until it slightly protrudes over the top of the cone. Round into domes.

2 Place a skewer into the center of each dome, compact the cake pop dough around the skewer, and refrigerate for 20 minutes.

3 Melt the candy melts (see page 220) to dipping consistency. Transfer to a tall container (I like to use plastic cups for dipping tall pops).

4 Once the pops are firm, use the skewer as a handle to dip the pops, completely covering the entire pop. Anchor the skewers in a block of floral foam or Styrofoam and let the pops set.

5 Once dry, support the top of the dome with two fingers while gently twisting the skewer loose, removing it from the "carrot."

6 Dip the stem of a mint sprig into some additional melted candy and insert into the waiting skewer hole. Try to get the mint stem to go into the cake pop as far as possible so you have a good "handle" with which to pick up the carrot.

7 Pour the cookie crumbs into a long, thin container, add the carrots with the tops just poking out of the ground, and allow the guests to pick their own "veggies."

Lemon Curd
CHEESECAKE EGGS

YOU'LL NEED

8 ounces cream cheese, at room temperature

1 can (14 ounces) sweetened condensed milk

2 teaspoons finely grated lemon zest (from 2 lemons)

¼ cup lemon juice

12 hollow white chocolate Easter eggs (2½ inches tall), store-bought or homemade (recipe follows)

¼ cup lemon curd

1 In a large mixer bowl, beat the cream cheese until smooth. Beat in the condensed milk until smooth. Add the lemon zest and juice and beat again until smooth and creamy. Refrigerate for 1 hour.

2 Gently knock the top off the Easter eggs to create a small opening, giving it a cracked shell effect.

3 Place the cheesecake mixture into a piping bag, snip off a ½-inch opening, and pipe the cheesecake into the eggs to just below the rim. (You will have leftover cheesecake filling; it can be frozen for up to a month.) Refrigerate the eggs for 1 hour.

4 Scoop a small well in the center with a teaspoon, fill with 1 teaspoon lemon curd, and tap gently on a work surface to flatten (to look like the yolk in the center of the egg).

HOMEMADE WHITE CHOCOLATE EASTER EGGS

Melt 9 ounces white candy melts (see page 220). Paint a layer into a chocolate mold that makes Easter eggs about 2½ inches tall by 1½ inches wide. Set in the fridge, then paint a second coat of melted candy. Return to the fridge. Remove the eggs from the mold. Heat a small skillet over medium heat. Lightly touch the rims of two egg halves onto the hot surface for 3 seconds so they just start to melt, then quickly press the melted edges together. You will need 12 eggs total.

Fresh Picked

STRAWBERRY
BASKETS

MAKES 6 BASKETS

YOU'LL NEED

5 ounces milk chocolate
2 pounds small strawberries
1 ounce white chocolate
6 cardboard berry baskets

1 Melt the milk chocolate (see page 220) to dipping consistency.

2 Using the cap as a handle, gently dip each strawberry in the milk chocolate to halfway up the berry. Place the berry onto parchment paper to set.

3 Melt the white chocolate and use a toothpick to place small seed-size dots neatly over the strawberries.

4 Fill the berry baskets with the chocolate-dipped strawberries.

Carrot, Orange, and Ginger
JUICE

MAKES 6 SERVINGS

YOU'LL NEED

8 oranges, peeled
10 carrots, ends trimmed, cut up
1-inch piece fresh ginger
6 (7-ounce) milk bottles
1 bunch of fresh mint
Green straws, trimmed to 1 inch above the bottle lip

Place the oranges, carrots, and ginger in a juicer and juice. Pour into the milk bottles. Place a sprig of mint into each straw to serve.

TIME SAVER: *If you're not into juicing or don't have much time, just make (or buy) orange juice.*

Strawberry Mojito
MOCKTAILS

MAKES 6 SERVINGS

YOU'LL NEED

½ cup sugar

1 cup hot water

2 cups coarsely chopped strawberries (about 12 ounces)

Strips of zest from 2 lemons (peeled with a vegetable peeler)

1 cup fresh lemon juice

2 cups cold water

6 (16-ounce) glasses

1 bunch fresh mint leaves

1 liter lemon-lime soda (such as Sprite)

Lemon wheels, lime wheels, fresh mint, and strawberries

Decorative straws

1 In a medium saucepan, combine the sugar and hot water and stir over medium heat until the sugar is completely dissolved. Add the strawberries and lemon zest to the hot liquid and remove from the heat. Set aside to cool completely.

2 Pour the cooled syrup and berries into a fine sieve set over a pitcher or drink dispenser. With the back of a spoon or a rubber spatula, squish the berries to extract most of the syrup. Discard the solids.

3 Add the lemon juice and cold water to the syrup mixture and stir until well blended.

4 Divide evenly among the glasses. Add 6 large mint leaves and lots of ice to each glass. Top with lemon-lime soda.

5 Add a few strawberry pieces to each glass, place a lemon wheel and lime wheel on the rim of each glass, and garnish with mint and a straw.

TIME SAVER: *The base mix (minus the mint, ice, and soda) can be refrigerated for up to 1 week before serving.*

PICKET FENCE

YOU'LL NEED

Picket Fence template (page 224)

White craft paper

Scissors

Ruler or measuring tape

Square or rectangular vase

Thin double-sided tape

Thin white ribbon

GET CRAFTY

1 Trace the Picket Fence template to use as a guide to cut pickets from white craft paper. Measure the vase and cut out as many pickets as you need to reach all the way around your vase.

2 Wrap the vase all the way around with two lines of double-sided tape (spacing them about the same distance apart as the horizontal supports on a picket fence). Stick white ribbon to the tape.

3 Place a strip of double-sided tape on the back of each picket and affix the pickets all the way around the vase.

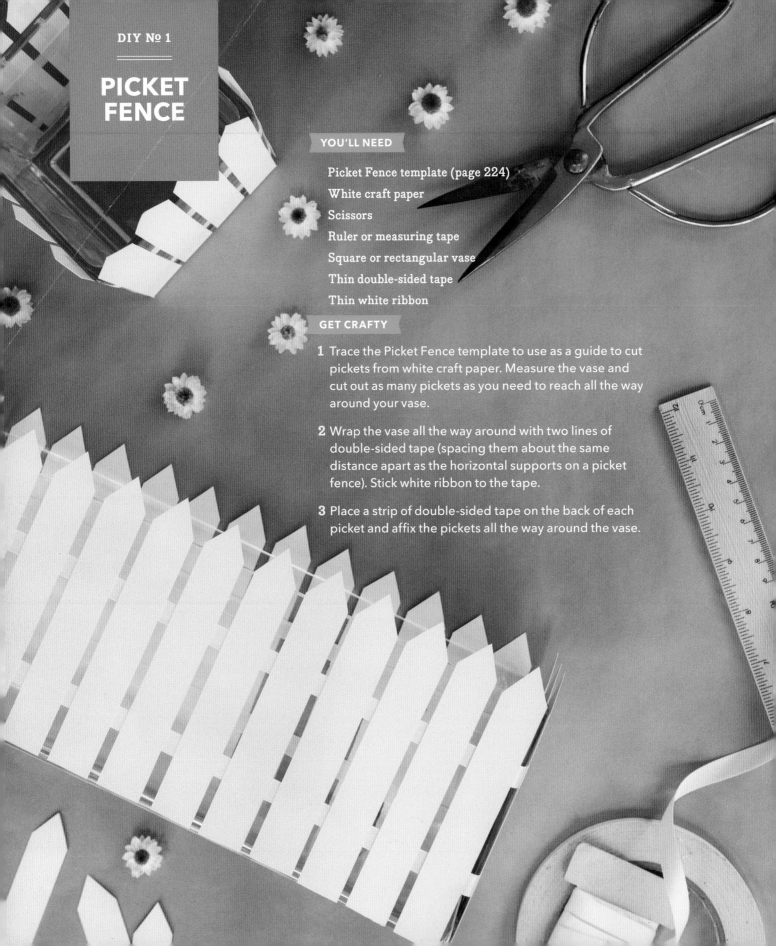

FLOWERPOT CAKE STANDS

YOU'LL NEED

Lace or doilies

Terra-cotta flowerpots in different shapes and sizes

Paper

Acrylic spray paint

Strong glue (I use an epoxy)

Flowerpot saucers or plates and platters (check your local thrift store!)

GET CRAFTY

1 Once your materials are assembled **A**, take a piece of lace and lay it over a section of your terra-cotta pot—you can slightly dampen the lace a little to help it stick to the pot **B**.

2 Using a piece of paper to protect the rest of your pot, spray over the lace. Allow to set for 5 minutes, then peel away the lace.

3 Turn the flowerpot upside down and place a generous amount of glue on the bottom. Place a flowerpot saucer, plate, or platter on the glue **C** and weight it down with a couple of books, allowing to set overnight.

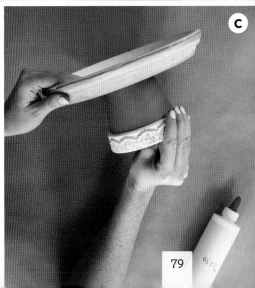

79

I displayed my creations on two ladders with worn wooden planks running between them for an interesting take on a dessert table. I love the way the desserts are stacked layer upon layer, with cake stands and crates providing different heights within each layer.

SPRING
PARTY

GREENERY IS an absolute must at a spring party, as are white picket fences, garden-inspired dishes, and bright colors.

Of course, any spring party simply *has* to have fresh flowers. Why not ask each of the guests to contribute a bunch of blooms so you get a great variety with a personal touch!

In addition to the greenery, flowers, and gorgeous garden backdrop, I also bought some potted herbs to add more green to my display and used them to replenish my herb garden when the party was over.

Spring is a magical time of year for so many reasons. Winter's over, the air is warming up, baby animals are everywhere, and the outdoors is becoming a viable entertaining option for the first time in months.

Fresh flavors, garden themes, pastel colors, and an outdoor setting are the key ingredients to a great spring party. Whether you're entertaining for Easter, hosting a shower, or just getting together with friends, there's never a better time to entertain than spring!

TEA
FOR TWO

"Make a Splash"
DRIP
CAKE

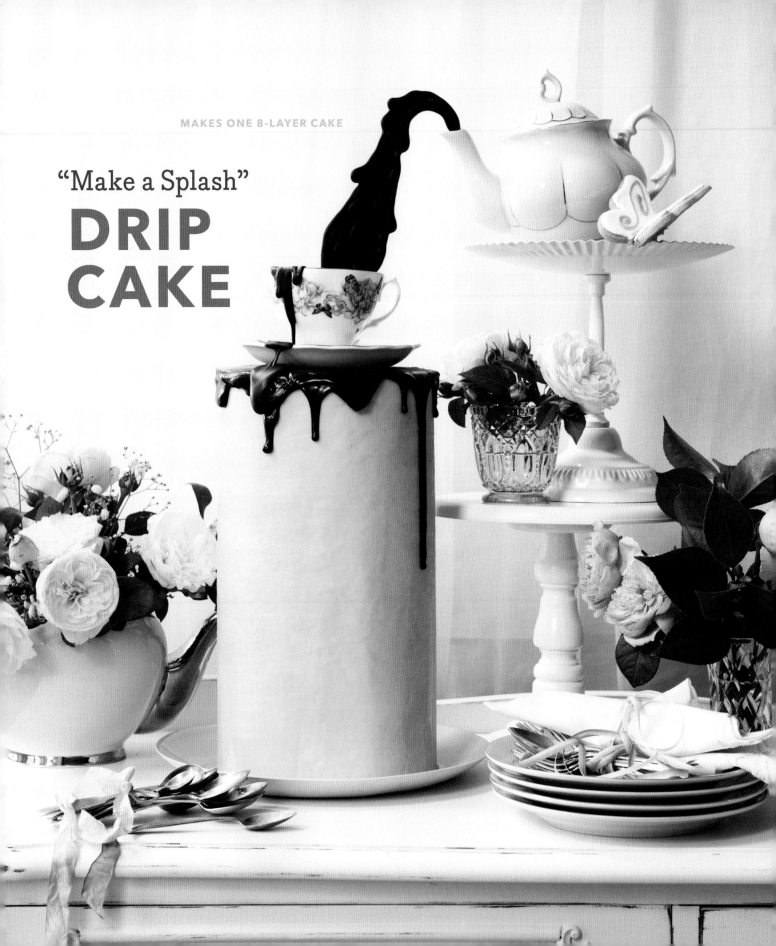

2 batches Rich Chocolate Mud Cake batter (page 211)

3 batches Vanilla Bean Buttercream Frosting (page 215)

Green food coloring

8-inch cake board

5-inch thin cake board

½ batch Dark Chocolate Ganache (page 218)

Decorative teacup and saucer

Tea Spill template (page 224)

5 ounces dark chocolate candy melts

10- to 12-inch-diameter cake stand (about 8 inches high)

6-inch-diameter cake stand (about 8 inches high)

1 decorative teapot

2 or 3 marshmallows

1 Preheat the oven to 325°F. Grease and flour four 6 x 3-inch cake pans. Line the bottoms with rounds of parchment paper. (If you only have two pans, do this in batches, and do not mix up the second batch of batter until you're ready to bake the second set of cakes.)

2 Make the cake batter, scrape into the pans, and bake until a wooden skewer inserted into the center comes out clean, about 1¼ hours.

3 Make the buttercream frosting, adding a few drops of food coloring at the end to make a pastel green.

4 Carve and level the cakes (see page 222, step 1); reserve the offcuts. Halve each cake horizontally to make 8 layers total. Starting on the 8-inch cake board, stack, layer, and support (using the 5-inch cake board) the cake (see page 222, steps 2 and 3). Frost with the green frosting (see page 223, step 4). Refrigerate for 1 hour to set.

5 Make the ganache to pouring consistency.

6 Take the reserved cake offcuts and use a round cookie cutter to cut rounds of cake that will fit inside the teacup. Place a round of cake in the teacup, top with a layer of ganache, then another round of cake, and keep going until the cup still has ¼ inch of space at the top. Set aside.

7 Remove the green cake from the fridge and check the temperature of your ganache—it should not feel hot. Place 6 tablespoons of the ganache on top of the cake and immediately use an offset spatula to spread it to the outside edges of the cake, allowing it to drip over the sides a little **A** .

8 Trace the Tea Spill template onto a sheet of parchment. Melt the candy melts (see page 220) and place in a zip-seal bag, cutting off a small corner. Pipe around the outside edges of the shape and let set. Then cut a slightly larger tip from the bag and fill in the shape completely, making sure the melted candy is quite thick **B** . Allow the "tea spill" to set at room temperature.

9 Glue the teacup to the saucer with a little dab of melted candy. (Reserve the remaining melted candy.) Place the teacup saucer onto the cake, directly onto the ganache **C** . Drizzle a little ganache over the edge of the saucer and teacup as though the tea has spilled out of the teacup. Set aside to set at room temperature. Meanwhile, place the "tea spill" into the fridge for 15 minutes.

10 Use a knife to cut a 1-inch slit in the center of the "cake" in the teacup. Insert the "tea spill," thick side down, into the slit in the teacup cake until it touches the bottom of the cup **D** .

11 This last part must be done once the cake is in its final position. Once positioned, place the 10-inch cake stand right beside it. Use a little melted candy on the base of the 6-inch cake stand and "glue" it onto the larger stand.

12 Place a small spot of melted candy on the base of the teapot, in line with the spout. Line up the open end of the teapot spout with the thin tip of the "tea spill" so the chocolate is just touching the spout and set the teapot on the top cake stand in that position. Place one or more marshmallows underneath the teapot to help support the slightly raised base (cut them to size if required).

> **MONEY SAVER:** *If you don't have multiple cake stands, use a stack of books covered in vintage craft paper to replace the bottom cake stand.*

Floating
BUTTERFLY
COOKIES

MAKES 30 BUTTERFLIES

YOU'LL NEED	1 batch Vanilla Sugar Cookie dough (page 214)
	Butterfly cookie cutter (3-inch wingspan)
	5 ounces white candy melts
	5 ounces pale pink candy melts

1 Make the cookie dough and chill as directed.

2 Preheat the oven to 350°F. Line the baking sheets with parchment paper.

3 Working with one portion of dough at a time, generously flour the work surface and roll out the dough to a ⅛-inch thickness. Cut out butterfly shapes. Then use a sharp knife to cut each butterfly in half down the middle of the body.

4 Place the cookies in pairs onto the baking sheets and bake until the edges just start to turn golden brown, 7 to 10 minutes. Immediately transfer the cookies to a wire rack in pairs to cool completely.

5 Fold a 12-inch length of foil in half lengthwise and in half again lengthwise. Fold down the middle to create a crease and then place like a wide "V" (wide side up) down one side of an empty egg carton. Repeat with another piece of foil and set over the other half of the egg carton.

6 Melt the white candy melts (see page 220) and place into a piping bag fitted with a #1 plain tip.

7 Pipe a thin white border around half of the butterfly pairs. Allow to set slightly before filling in the borders to completely cover.

8 Repeat the procedure with the pink candy melts on the other half of the butterflies.

9 Once the white base has set, with the pink candy melts still in a piping bag fitted with a #1 plain tip, pipe small swirls on the wings of the white butterflies. Repeat with the white candy melts on the pink butterflies.

10 Flatten the foil "V," take 2 butterfly halves and lay together on the foil with the colored sides facing up and the center crease of the foil "V" running between the two halves. Pipe a line of candy melts in between each pair, making a long "butterfly body" down the join. Lift the foil and cookies, gently placing it back into its "V" shape in the egg carton support so the butterflies look as though they are in flight.

11 Allow to set at room temperature. Once set, remove from the egg carton to reveal floating butterflies.

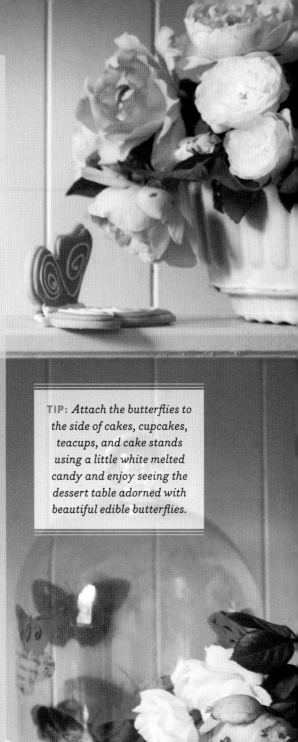

TIP: *Attach the butterflies to the side of cakes, cupcakes, teacups, and cake stands using a little white melted candy and enjoy seeing the dessert table adorned with beautiful edible butterflies.*

GARDEN TEACUP CAKES

with edible flowers

MAKES 24 CUPCAKES

YOU'LL NEED

1 batch Classic Vanilla
Cake batter (page 208)

¾ cup white chocolate
chips

1 bag (12 ounces)
frozen unsweetened
raspberries (about 2
cups)

Teacups and saucers

1 batch White Chocolate
Ganache (page 219)

Edible flowers, such as
pansies, nasturtiums,
and violets

1 Preheat the oven to 350°F. Line 24 cups of muffin tins
with paper liners.

2 Make the cupcake batter and gently fold in the
chocolate chips. Spoon the batter into the muffin
cups, filling them two-thirds full. Add 4 raspberries
to the top of each cupcake.

3 Bake until the centers spring back when touched,
20 to 22 minutes. Check first at 18 minutes, then
each minute thereafter. Cool the cupcakes in the
tin for 5 minutes, then remove to a wire rack to cool
completely. Place the cooled cupcakes into teacups.

4 Make the ganache to whipped consistency. Place
it in a piping bag fitted with a plain piping tip. Pipe
a medium swirl onto the cupcakes and top with
assorted blooms.

5 Serve on saucers.

> **TIP:** *Mix up the flowers so no two cupcakes are
> the same, and use mismatched teacups and saucers for
> a true vintage high tea effect.*
>
> **MONEY SAVER:** *You don't have to have all the
> cupcakes in teacups; just a few among the display is
> enough to make this look pop.*

MERINGUES
À LA ROSE

strawberry and lemon

MAKES TWELVE 2-INCH SANDWICH COOKIES

4 extra-large egg whites, at room temperature

1 cup plus 2 tablespoons (220g) superfine sugar

2 teaspoons cornstarch, sifted

1 teaspoon distilled white vinegar

Pink food coloring

Yellow food coloring

½ batch White Chocolate Ganache (page 219)

Strawberry essence

1 tablespoon finely grated lemon zest

About 6 green candy straps

1 Preheat the oven to 215°F (these cook low and slow). Line a baking sheet with parchment paper.

2 Beat the egg whites in a clean, dry bowl with an electric mixer on high speed until soft peaks form. Gradually add the sugar in thirds, beating well after each addition. Continue beating until the mixture is glossy and it ribbons from the end of the beaters when lifted, then beat about 2 minutes longer.

3 Add the cornstarch and vinegar and beat until just combined.

4 Split into two bowls and add pink food coloring to one bowl and yellow to the other. Mix the color through but not entirely: You want to be able to see white streaks in the meringue mixture.

5 Place the pink mixture into a clean, dry piping bag fitted with a 1M open star tip. Starting in the center, pipe a low 2-inch-diameter swirl onto the lined baking sheet: The piping tip will do all the work for you, creating a beautiful rose pattern. Make 12 even-size roses until you've used all the meringue mixture. Repeat with the yellow meringue to make 12 yellow roses.

6 Bake until the meringue roses are completely dry when tapped on the base and come off the baking sheet with no resistance, about 2½ hours.

7 Remove from the oven and leave the meringues to dry out overnight.

8 Make the ganache. Split the ganache mixture into two bowls. Add 3 drops of pink food coloring and 3 drops of strawberry essence into one bowl and mix. Add the grated lemon zest and 4 drops of yellow food coloring to the other bowl and mix.

9 Pour each mixture into a separate zip-seal bag and place in the fridge for 15 minutes to partially set.

10 Cut small leaf shapes (about 1 inch long) out of candy straps and set aside.

11 Once the fillings are still soft enough to squeeze but are no longer runny, snip a small corner off each bag. Pipe a disk of strawberry filling on the flat side of a pink meringue rose, stick a leaf into the edge of the filling, and sandwich a second pink meringue rose over the leaf and filling.

12 Repeat with the lemon filling and yellow meringue roses.

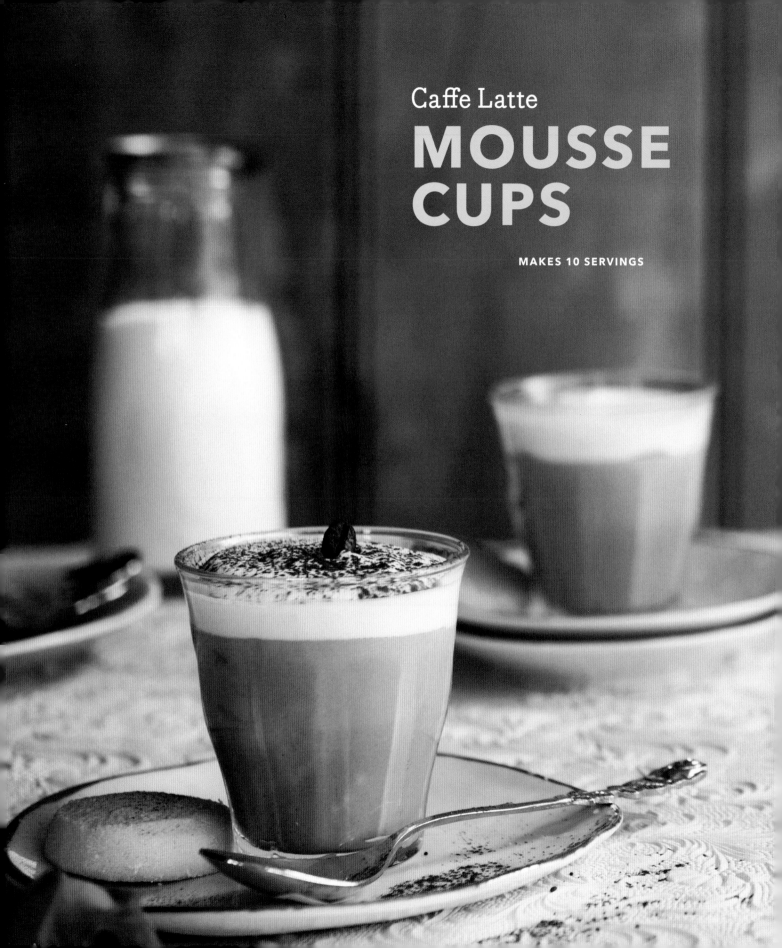

Caffe Latte
MOUSSE CUPS

MAKES 10 SERVINGS

YOU'LL NEED

1 tablespoon instant coffee
¼ cup boiling water
3½ ounces milk chocolate, chopped
2½ cups heavy cream
10 (3-ounce) espresso glasses
Coffee beans and cocoa powder

1 In a small bowl, stir the coffee and boiling water to dissolve. Refrigerate until cold.

2 Melt the milk chocolate with ¼ cup of the heavy cream and stir to form a ganache.

3 Using an electric mixer, whip the remaining 2¼ cups heavy cream until soft peaks start to form. Be careful not to overwhip. Set aside and refrigerate half of the whipped cream.

4 Using a spatula and large sweeping motions, gently fold the ganache and cooled coffee into the remaining whipped cream, until combined.

5 Divide the mousse mixture among the espresso glasses, leaving a ½-inch gap at the top of each glass. Refrigerate for 1 hour.

6 Once the mousse is set, spoon the reserved whipped cream on top, filling to just below the glass rim.

7 Decorate the top of the mousse with a coffee bean and a sprinkling of cocoa powder.

COCKTAIL TRIFLES

MAKES 12 SERVINGS

YOU'LL NEED

1 box (3 ounces) strawberry Jell-O

12 (12-ounce) glasses or glass bowls

4 tablespoons chopped strawberries

2 tablespoons salted butter, melted

3 cups coarsely crushed shortbread
   cookies (10½ ounces)

¾ cup strawberry jam or jelly

2 cups raspberries

1 cup blueberries

1 box (3.4 ounces) vanilla instant
   pudding mix

2 cups cold milk

Whipped cream, for serving

1 Make the Jell-O according to the package directions and divide evenly among the glasses; each glass gets 3 tablespoons. Place 1 teaspoon strawberries into each glass and place in the fridge for 2 hours to set.

2 In a bowl, stir together the butter and shortbread crumbs. The mixture should resemble loosely held together chunky cookies. Divide the cookie mixture evenly among the glasses. Each glass gets ¼ cup of cookies.

3 Place 1 tablespoon of jam in each glass and spread using the back of a spoon, trying not to disturb the cookie mixture too much.

4 Cover the jam layer with raspberries and blueberries, placing the fruit up against the sides of the glasses.

5 Make the pudding mix according to the package directions, using the cold milk. Immediately pour into a piping bag with no tip.

6 Starting in the center of the glass so as not to disturb the berries, pipe pudding into each glass, dividing evenly among the glasses (about 3 tablespoons per glass). Tap each glass on the counter to ensure the pudding has settled.

7 Refrigerate for at least 15 minutes to set the pudding. Serve topped with raspberries and blueberries, with whipped cream on the side.

Rose and Lime
SPRITZERS

MAKES 6 SERVINGS

6 limes
6 fragrant pink roses
2 tablespoons rose water
1 liter lemon-lime soda (such as Sprite)
1 liter club soda
Lime wheels

1 Juice 3 of the limes and cut the remaining 3 limes into thin wedges. Remove the petals from the roses and rinse under cold water.

2 Combine the lime juice and rose water in a 3-quart pitcher and stir.

3 Add the lemon-lime soda, club soda, half of the lime wedges, and half of the rose petals and stir gently.

4 To serve, place a small amount of ice in each of 6 tall glasses. Follow with a lime wedge, a rose petal, more ice, another lime wedge, and rose petal. Top with more ice.

5 Fill with the rose spritzer mix and top with a single rose petal and a lime wheel.

Layered
FRUIT SMOOTHIES

YOU'LL NEED

4 cups frozen raspberries
4½ cups vanilla frozen yogurt
6 champagne flutes
8 ounces (1 cup) blueberries
Decorative straws

1 In a blender, combine the raspberries and 3 cups of the frozen yogurt and blend until smooth. Spoon evenly into the champagne flutes, filling each flute just over halfway. Refrigerate for 30 minutes.

2 Meanwhile, combine the blueberries and remaining 1½ cups frozen yogurt in a blender and blend until smooth.

3 Gently spoon the blueberry mixture over the raspberry mixture, filling the champagne flute to ½ inch below the rim. Refrigerate for 15 minutes.

4 To serve, garnish with a straw. Serve immediately.

CAKE STANDS

GET CRAFTY

1 Place a generous amount of epoxy on the top of your base option.

2 Lay your plate upside down, place the glued end of the base into the center of the bottom of the plate, and allow to set for 6 to 12 hours.

YOU'LL NEED

Glue (I use epoxy)

Base options: cups, candlesticks, or upturned wineglasses

Assorted plates and platters

TIP: *I love making my own cake stands. Anytime I'm in a thrift store or I see items on sale, I stock up on base options and interesting sizes and shapes of plates. For bases, think candlesticks, upturned glasses, and teacups. And for plates, anything goes! The more unusual, the better in my opinion.*

GLUE

PAPER ROSETTES

Colored craft paper

Ruler

String or ribbon

Double-sided tape

GET CRAFTY

1 Fold the craft paper over in a backward and forward motion like an accordion, using the ruler as a guide for even folds **A**.

2 Place two of these pieces together, tie a piece of string around the center, and secure **B**.

3 Open up to reveal a series of beautiful fans **C** and use double-sided tape to secure the sides together to make one single rosette.

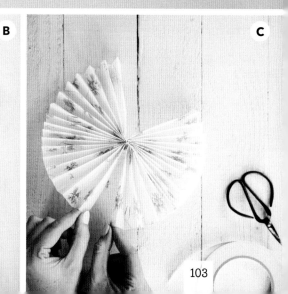

A

B

C

103

If you have an old ornate dresser, this is a great excuse to clear it out and use it to display the desserts in a totally unique way. Desserts can go in drawers, cakes in cubbyholes, and lots of hidden spaces can be used to stash sweet treats, fresh flowers, and beautiful decorations.

TEA
PARTY

FRESH FLOWERS are a must for any high tea: Split the bunches and create smaller flower accents in more places and be bold with colors and scents here. There's nothing better than the smell of lilies or jasmine wafting through the air.

First, you'll need teacups, but matching sets are definitely not required. Grab any tea-related accessories from thrift stores, friends' houses, and your grandma's place in the weeks before the party and lay them all out in a beautiful, dainty, floral organized mishmash of everything pretty.

High tea is a great way to get everyone together and step outside of your normal routine. Whether you're celebrating Mother's Day, throwing a shower for a friend, or you just want an excuse to break out the dainty desserts on a weekend, a party inspired by high tea is elegant, classy, and so full of sweet mini delights it's hard not to see the cuteness of every bite.

THE **GRILL** MASTER

HOT DOG CAKE

with pouring
ketchup illusion

MAKES 1 LARGE HOT DOG AND
BUN WITH A SIDE OF FRIES

1 batch White Chocolate Mud Cake batter (page 210)

1 batch White Chocolate Ganache (page 219)

Yellow food coloring

Brown food coloring

½ batch Red Velvet Cake Pop Dough (page 212)

Ketchup Pour template (page 227)

7 ounces red candy melts

1 takeout ketchup packet, emptied, cleaned, and dried

7 ounces green candy melts

2 cups cornflakes

1 cup granulated sugar

½ teaspoon ground cinnamon

1. Preheat the oven to 325°F. Grease and flour a 9½ x 5½-inch loaf pan and a 6 x 3-inch round cake pan. Line the bottoms of both pans with parchment paper.

2. Make the cake batter. Place 5⅓ cups batter into the loaf pan, and the remaining 2⅔ cups into the round (or square) pan. Bake until a wooden skewer inserted into the center of each cake comes out clean; 45 minutes for the round pan and 1¼ hours for the loaf. Cool the cakes in the pans for 15 minutes, then invert onto a wire rack to cool. Turn the loaf right side up to cool. Wrap the cooled 6-inch cake in plastic wrap and place in the fridge.

3. Use a small serrated knife to round off the edges of the loaf cake and create a hot dog bun shape, making it as smooth as possible. Slice a 1-inch-deep "V" groove along the top of the "bun" (like a split-top bun) to make room for the hot dog **A**.

4. Line a baking pan with waxed paper and top with a wire rack. Place the "hot dog bun" on the rack.

5. Make the ganache to pouring consistency. Measure out ½ cup, tint with 3 to 4 drops of yellow food coloring (this will be the mustard), and set aside.

6. Tint the remaining ganache with a little brown food coloring, adding a drop at a time, to a soft caramel color. If the ganache is looking too "dirty brown," add a drop of yellow to make it a more caramel color.

7. While the caramel-colored ganache is still warm, pour over the entire "hot dog bun," **B** tilting the rack so the ganache doesn't pool in the "V." Refrigerate the cake on the rack until set. Scrape the ganache that landed in the baking sheet back into a bowl, but remove any noticeable crumbs.

8. Once the first layer of ganache has set, reheat the caramel ganache to pouring consistency and pour a second coat onto the cake to add an additional smoother layer. Refrigerate to set.

9. Roll the cake pop dough into a long sausage, slightly longer than the "bun." Wrap the sausage tightly in parchment to create a cylinder **C**. Freeze for 30 minutes. Use a knife to round the ends of the cake pop roll to resemble a hot dog.

10. Trace the Ketchup Pour template on parchment. Melt the red candy melts (see page 220) and place in a zip-seal bag; snip off a small corner. Pipe an outline around the "ketchup pour." Fill in, making it nice and thick, as it needs to be strong. Lay the ketchup packet on the still-wet candy melts, covering the corner slightly. Allow to set at room temperature, then refrigerate.

11. Melt the green candy melts in a medium bowl. Gently fold in the cornflakes to coat. Spread on parchment to set, then gently break into cornflake "relish."

12. Carefully transfer the hot dog bun cake to a rectangular tray. Lay some "relish" along the inside of the bun. Lay the cake pop "hot dog" in the center. Let the cake come to room temperature.

13. Peel the paper off the "ketchup pour." Two to three inches in from the end of the "hot dog," use a knife to make a slit through the "hot dog" all the way to the bottom of the "bun." Gently insert the "ketchup pour" into the slit **D**.

14. Remelt the remaining red candy melts and place in a zip-seal bag. Draw a ketchup squiggle along the length of the "hot dog," starting at the point where the ketchup illusion entered the hot dog. Pipe a squiggle of ganache "mustard" next to the ketchup.

15. **To make "fries":** Slice the round cake crosswise into ½-inch slices and then cut each slice into "fries" (use a crinkle cutter if you have one). In a bowl, combine the sugar and cinnamon. Drop the fries a few at a time into the sugar and roll them around to coat.

WAFFLE PIZZAS

MAKES 4 TO 6 PIZZAS (16 TO 24 SLICES)

YOU'LL NEED

1 batch Seven-Minute Frosting (page 217)
Red food coloring
1 batch Classic Vanilla Cake batter (page 208)
1-inch round cookie cutter

TOPPINGS:

White candy melts (for mozzarella)
Red fruit roll (for pepperoni)
Chocolate-covered almonds (for whole olives)
Green gummy Lifesavers (for sliced jalapeños)
Yellow Starburst candies, trimmed to long triangles (for pineapple)
Pink Starburst candies, trimmed to ⅛-inch pieces (for ham)

1 Make the frosting and tint it to look like pizza sauce.

2 Make the cake batter.

3 Preheat a round Belgian waffle maker and coat generously with cooking spray.

4 Spoon the batter into the waffle maker (if you have the option, select the lightest browning setting). Allow to cook for 4 minutes before checking if the waffle is done. Test by lightly touching the center: The waffle should spring back.

5 Allow the waffle to completely cool in the maker before removing.

6 **Make the toppings:** Grate the candy melts using a grater to resemble mozzarella. Open a red fruit roll and use the cookie cutter to cut "slices" of "pepperoni."

7 Using an offset spatula, spread the frosting over the cooled waffles, leaving a slight gap around the edges for the "crust."

8 For a traditional supreme pizza, top with the "pepperoni," "mozzarella," "olives," and "jalapeños." For a Hawaiian pizza, top with "mozzarella," "ham," and "pineapple."

KIDS IN THE KITCHEN: *Gather all the ingredients and let the kids decorate the pizzas themselves.*

TACO COOKIES

MAKES 8 TO 10 TACOS

COOKIES:

- 4 extra-large egg whites
- 1 teaspoon vanilla extract
- 1 cup (125g) all-purpose flour
- 1 cup (190g) superfine sugar

TOPPINGS:

- 25 chocolate sandwich cookies
- 6 tablespoons salted butter, melted
- 2 cups shredded coconut (see Note)
- Green food coloring
- 30 yellow Starburst candies
- Red M&M's (for cherry tomatoes)

1 **Make the cookies:** Preheat the oven to 400°F. Line a baking sheet with parchment paper. Draw two 5-inch circles on the parchment and flip over the parchment. Generously coat the parchment with cooking spray.

2 Cover a 1-inch-diameter tube or large dowel with parchment and tape to secure. You'll need this to be about 12 inches long. Prop the tube up at both ends using two tall cans or containers.

3 In a large bowl, whisk the egg whites, vanilla, flour, and sugar.

4 Spoon 1½ tablespoons of batter into each of the two 5-inch circles and use a spoon to create a 5-inch round. Tap the baking sheet on the counter to neaten the edges of the rounds.

5 Bake just until the edges of the cookies begin to brown, 5 to 7 minutes. Immediately loosen the cookies from the baking sheet by carefully pulling the parchment off the cookies and drape the cookies over the tube so the edges of the cookies are hanging freely. They will harden within 1 minute, so work quickly. Repeat with the remaining batter to make more cookies.

6 **Make the toppings:** Lightly crush the chocolate cookies so they are in small chunks (to resemble ground beef) and stir in the butter. Refrigerate for 15 minutes.

7 Place the coconut and 5 or 6 drops of food coloring into a zip-seal bag and shake vigorously until the coconut has turned completely green. Set the "lettuce" aside.

8 Cut the Starbursts into ⅛-inch-thick lengths (scissors work best here) to resemble shredded cheese.

To assemble, compress a small handful of cookie "beef" and place in the bottom of a cookie taco shell. Top with coconut "lettuce," M&M's "tomatoes," and Starburst "cheese."

> **TIP:** *Bake these in batches of two, otherwise you won't have time to hang them before they set.*

NOTES: *If you don't like the taste of coconut, you can make "lettuce" by stirring 1 cup of cornflakes with ¼ cup green melted candy. Allow to set before coarsely breaking apart.*

If you have taco racks, they're a huge help when it comes to serving these sweet treats.

KIDS IN THE KITCHEN: *Why not make a "stuff-it-yourself taco station" and let the kids make their taco cookies!*

117

BUCKET O' CHICKEN

½ batch Chocolate Cake Pop Dough (page 212)
6 cups cornflakes
14 ounces white candy melts
24 mini marshmallows
6 pretzel rods, halved
3½ ounces milk chocolate chips

1 Make the cake pop dough.

2 Loosely crush the cornflakes in a zip-seal bag using a rolling pin.

3 Melt the candy melts (see page 220) in a tall container or cup. Use a toothpick to apply a little of the melted candy to each of two mini marshmallows and glue them, pressing to adhere, at the top of one uncut end of a pretzel rod (like the end of a drumstick bone). Let set at room temperature.

4 Once set, dip the pretzel and marshmallows together into the melted candy to coat halfway. Tap off excess and refrigerate until firmly set.

5 Divide the cake pop dough into 12 equal pieces, each about the size of a golf ball.

6 Dip the uncoated (cut) end of the pretzel stick 2 inches into the melted candy and press the cake pop dough onto the pretzel, fashioning it into the shape of a chicken drumstick. Return to the refrigerator until firmly set.

7 Once all the drumsticks are firmly set, melt the chocolate chips and add to the remaining white melted candy to create a light brown chocolate.

8 Dip the "meat" part of the drumstick into the brown chocolate and immediately sprinkle with the crushed cornflakes—to make it look like fried chicken! Place on parchment paper and refrigerate until firmly set before stacking in a large bucket to serve.

TIP: *If you can find a clean, unused cardboard chicken bucket from a local takeout place, it helps take the presentation to the next level.*

"Beer"
JELL-O JIGGLERS
(NONALCOHOLIC)

MAKES 12 SERVINGS

YOU'LL NEED

2 cups apple juice

4 teaspoons unflavored gelatin powder

¼ cup water

12 shot glasses

½ cup sweetened condensed milk

1 In a small saucepan, bring the apple juice to a boil, then pour into a 4-cup measuring cup.

2 In a small bowl, stir the gelatin into the ¼ cup water until it resembles smooth applesauce. Add the gelatin to the measuring cup of hot apple juice and whisk to combine.

3 Divide the mixture among the glasses, stopping ¼ inch below the rim, and let set in the fridge for 2 to 3 hours.

4 To serve, use a teaspoon to spoon condensed milk on top of each glass to look like beer "foam."

TIP: *Try to find small beer steins or mini mason jar shot glasses to make your presentation even more realistic.*

12 Twinkies

6 lengths Haribo Strawberry Piccolos
(or other thick, round red licorice)

½ batch Seven-Minute Frosting (page 217)

Red food coloring

Yellow food coloring

1 green Twizzler

CAKE "FRIES":

1 store-bought pound cake

1 cup granulated sugar

½ teaspoon ground cinnamon

1 Using a serrated knife, make a lengthwise slice down the center of the Twinkie (like a split-top hot dog bun).

2 Trim the licorice to make "hot dogs" and place inside the Twinkie bun.

3 Place about two-thirds of the frosting into one bowl and the remaining frosting in a second bowl. Color the larger bowl red (for ketchup) and the other yellow (for mustard). Place each frosting into a separate zip-seal bag and snip off a small corner. Pipe a line of "mustard" and a line of "ketchup" onto each hot dog. (Reserve the remaining "ketchup" for serving with the fries.)

TWINKIE HOT DOGS

with pound cake fries

MAKES 12 "HOT DOGS"

4 Coarsely chop the Twizzler and sprinkle on as pickle relish.

5 Make the cake "fries": Slice the pound cake crosswise into ½-inch slices and then cut into "fries."

6 In a bowl, combine the sugar and cinnamon and stir well. Drop the fries a few at a time into the sugar mixture and roll them around to coat in the mixture.

7 Serve the "fries" beside the hot dogs, along with a small pot of frosting "ketchup" for dipping.

ROOT BEER FLOATS

MAKES 6 SERVINGS

6 (16-ounce) beer stein–style mugs
6 large scoops vanilla ice cream
2 liters root beer

1   Fill the mugs to just above halfway with root beer. Add 1 large scoop of ice cream.

2   Allow to foam for 3 minutes, then, if needed, drizzle a little more root beer over the top to bring the foam to just above the rim of the mug.

Mustachio
MILKSHAKES

MAKES 4 SERVINGS

YOU'LL NEED

Mustache template (page 227)
Black craft paper
4 flexible straws
4 cups whole milk
½ cup malted milk powder
1 pint vanilla ice cream
4 milkshake glasses
4 (3-inch) soft oatmeal raisin cookies

1 Trace the Mustache template and use as a guide to cut 4 mustaches from black craft paper. Use a hole punch to make a small hole in the center of each mustache and thread onto the bend of the straw.

2 In a blender, combine the milk, malted milk powder, and ice cream and blend until smooth. Divide the mixture among the glasses. Place a cookie on the work surface and gently force the bottom of the straw through the cookie (remove the plug of cookie from the straw).

3 Place the cookie and straw on top of the glass so the cookie acts like a lid.

TIME SAVER: *Make the mustache straws and poke the holes in the cookies in advance.*

These milkshakes are not only delicious, the mustaches make fabulous photo props on the day of your party.

125

BARBECUE TOOL RACKS

DAD

YOU'LL NEED

Water-based paint

Pegboard, cut to size (about 25 x 20 inches)

Chalkboard paint and chalk

Pegboard hooks

Assorted barbecue utensils

GET CRAFTY

1 Paint the pegboard in your desired color.

2 Once the board has dried, paint a rectangle of chalkboard paint in the top section of the board and allow to dry. This is for your personal message.

3 Add the pegboard hooks and barbecue utensils. Use chalk to write a message on the board.

TIP: *These look great hung as part of a party backdrop, or leaning up against a wall sitting on the table, but they're also functional and will last long after the party. This doubles as a gift idea for all the tools your grill master needs to hang.*

BARBECUE
CAKE STAND

YOU'LL NEED

Hacksaw

3 (12-inch) lengths
  1-inch wooden dowel

3 black-rubber leg tips

1 small cupboard handle

2 large bowls (see Note)

Heavy-duty glue (I use
  epoxy)

Red spray paint

1 (5-inch) plastic
  flowerpot saucer

Round wire rack or
  round pot stand rack

Black craft paper

GET CRAFTY

1 Once you assemble your materials , use a hacksaw or blade to cut one end of each piece of dowel to about a 22-degree angle. Affix the rubber tips to the uncut ends of the dowels.

2 Glue the cupboard handle to the top of one bowl.

3 Spray-paint the outside of the second bowl and allow to dry.

4 Place glue on the angle-cut ends of the dowels and glue them in a tripod pattern to the underside of the plastic flowerpot saucer B.

5 Scrunch up balls of black craft paper to resemble coals and fill the base, before placing the round wire rack on top C.

NOTE: *Get two bowls of matching size, around 12 inches across. For the wire rack, find one that will sit snugly in your bowl, to look like a grill grate.*

A

B

C

DAD'S TOOLS!

MENU
Hot Dog Cake
Waffle Pizzas
Cookie Tacos
Fried Chicken
CakePops
Twinkie-dogs
Jello Jigglers
Root Beer Floats
Mustachio
Milkshakes

I remember a brand of ketchup being released in monster green one year. I couldn't quite get used to eating something that was supposed to be red but was green. My eyes and my brain just didn't match, but when it hit my mouth, sure enough—ketchup!

You'll find this dessert table invokes those feelings of "Wait, this shouldn't taste like cake!" but you'll very soon get used to it and enjoy fooling all your guests with these imposter creations.

GRILL
MASTER
PARTY

WE SPEND most Saturdays entertaining, and BBQ is a way of life where I'm from. This is a bit of a twist on the usual meat and potato salad barbecue fare, and the real fun starts when people begin to realize they're looking at sweets disguised as savories.

This party was made to be hosted outdoors, making the perfect backdrop a rough, textured wall. Add pops of burlap, twine, and exposed metal for an element of texture throughout your dessert display.

I wanted a really strong barbecue feel for this party, so I opted for a traditional red-checkered tablecloth and really rustic accents. I added a little greenery and delightful fragrance with pots of fresh rosemary (which I later planted!) and stuck with red and yellow as my main color scheme.

A FRIGHTENING FEAST

CHAPTER
№

6

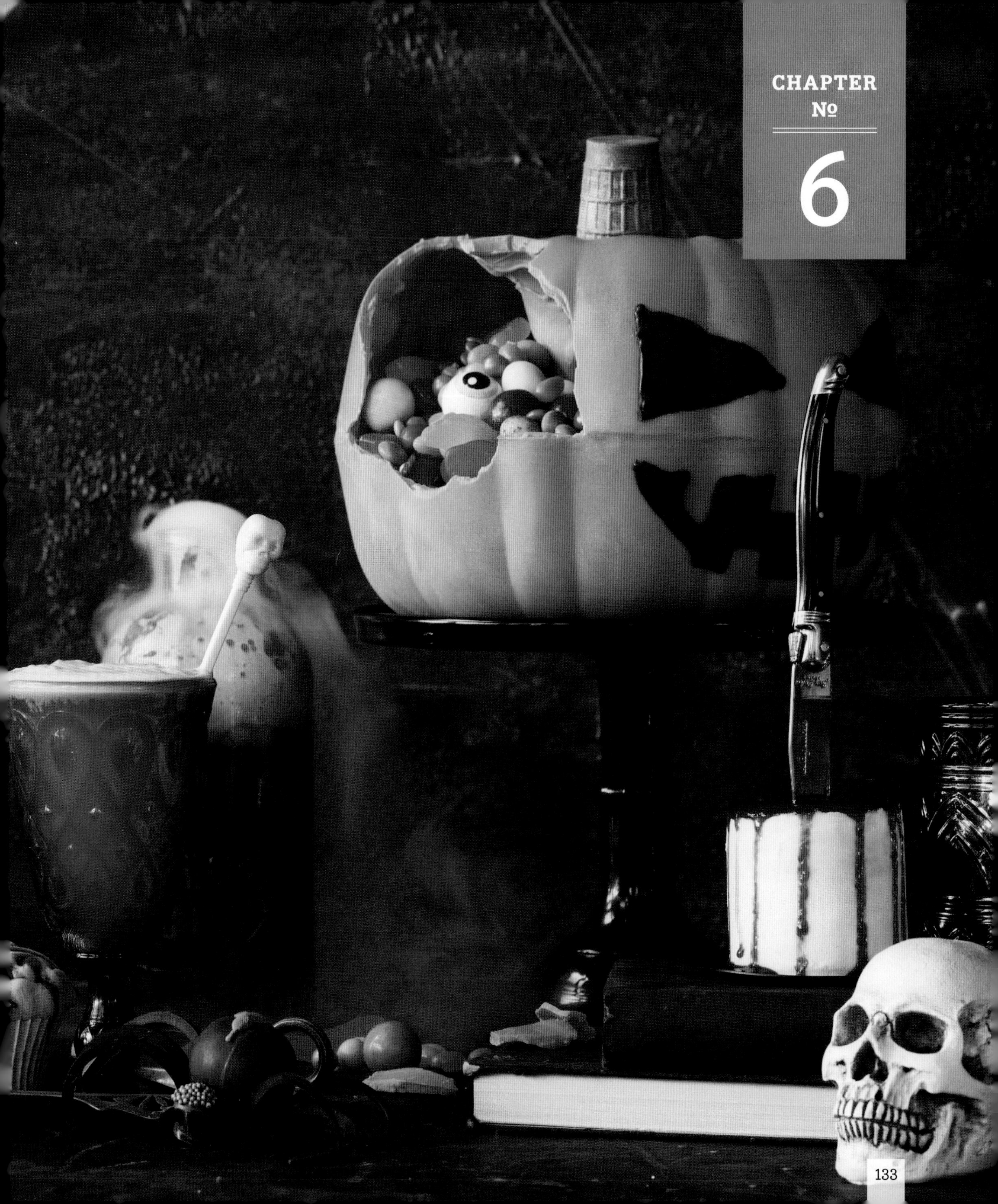

JACK O' LANTERN SMASH CAKE

MAKES 1 JACK O' LANTERN

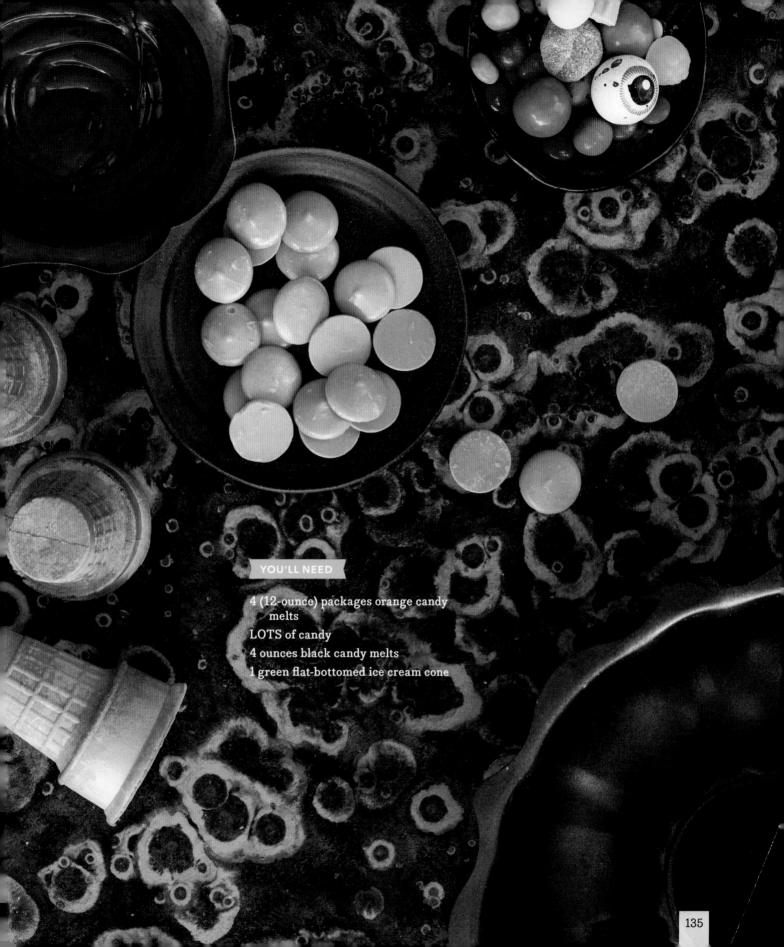

4 (12-ounce) packages orange candy
    melts
LOTS of candy
4 ounces black candy melts
1 green flat-bottomed ice cream cone

1   Melt 2 packages of the orange candy melts (see page 220) and pour half the melted candy into a 10- to 12-cup nonstick Bundt pan.

2   Use a spatula to evenly distribute the melted candy around the inside of the pan 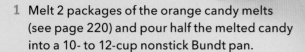 , up the sides, and up the center column. Refrigerate for 15 minutes (see Note), until set. Repeat with the remaining melted candy to make a second layer, ensuring there are no gaps. Refrigerate again until set. Once fully set, remove the candy shell from the Bundt pan.

3   Melt the remaining 2 packages of orange candy melts. Set aside about ¼ cup of melted candy for later. Use the remaining melted candy to create a second candy shell, making two coats and refrigerating as before so you have 2 completed pumpkin halves.

4   Apply a small amount of orange melted candy to a serving plate or cake board and use it to stick one of the candy shells, open side up, in place.

5   Fill the shell with lots of candy, building up as high as possible Ⓑ .

6   Put the reserved ¼ cup orange candy in a zip-seal bag, cut off a small corner, and pipe a thin line around the outside edge of the pumpkin shell Ⓒ . Place the remaining pumpkin shell on top and press to glue together.

7   Melt the black candy melts, place in a zip-seal bag, and draw a jack o' lantern face on the pumpkin Ⓓ . Let set.

8   Add the ice cream cone upside down in the center well to create a stalk. Smash and enjoy.

TIP: *If the candy shell at the center of the Bundt pan isn't easily coming loose, use a hair dryer to gently heat the middle of the pan (no more than 5 seconds at a time) and it should pull away.*

NOTE: *The shell needs the chill of the refrigerator in order for the chocolate to contract away from the sides of the pan.*

ZOMBIE BRAIN CUPCAKES

MAKES 24 CUPCAKES

1 batch Classic Vanilla Cake batter (page 208)

Green food coloring

1½ batches Vanilla Bean Buttercream Frosting (page 215)

2 cups strawberry sundae syrup

1 large jar morello cherries

Thin food-grade syringes (optional)

1 Preheat the oven to 350°F. Line 24 cups of 2 muffin tins with green cupcake liners.

2 Make the cake batter and tint it green. Fill each muffin cup two-thirds full with batter. Bake until the center springs back when lightly touched, 20 to 22 minutes.

3 Transfer to a wire rack to cool.

4 Make the frosting and tint it green.

5 Once the cupcakes are cooled, use a sharp knife to carve out a cone-shaped hole in the center of each cupcake, reserving the piece you cut out. Spoon in about 1 teaspoon of strawberry syrup, then fill with 2 or 3 cherries (whatever fits) and fill to the rim with syrup. Allow to sit for 5 minutes, as the cupcake will absorb some of the syrup, and then add more (skip this step if you are using the syringes; see step 8). Trim off the pointed bottom of the reserved core pieces and use the top as a lid, placing them back on top of the cupcake centers.

6 Scoop 1 tablespoon of frosting on top of each cupcake and use the back of the knife to create a smooth dome. Place the rest of the frosting into a zip-seal bag and cut off a small corner. Pipe two long center lines down the middle of the cupcake (this is the center of the brain where the two lobes meet) and then on either side, pipe two rows of curvy lines to resemble brain matter.

7 Using a teaspoon, allow small droplets of strawberry syrup to drop onto the tops of the zombie brains to resemble blood.

8 If using syringes, suck up some of the remaining strawberry syrup into the syringes and stab them into the tops of the cupcakes.

9 Encourage your guests to inject their "zombie brains" with strawberry "blood" just before eating.

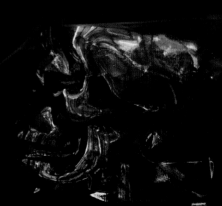

AXE MURDERER COOKIES

MAKES 20 KNIVES AND 20 BODIES

1 batch Vanilla Sugar Cookie dough (page 214),
   plus flour for rolling out
Knife and Body templates (page 226)
9 ounces black candy melts
7 ounces white candy melts
Tiny silver dragées (2mm)
4 ounces red candy melts

Make the cookie dough and chill as directed.

Preheat the oven to 350°F. Line 2 baking sheets with parchment paper.

Trace the Knife and Body onto a piece of thick paper and cut out to use as templates.

On a floured work surface, roll the chilled dough out to a ⅛-inch thickness. Place the templates onto the cookie dough and use a sharp knife to cut around the shapes. Reroll any scraps. Cut out an assortment of bodies and knives. Place the bodies and the knives on separate baking sheets.

Bake the cookies until the edges just start to turn golden brown, 7 to 10 minutes. Check both sheets separately as they will bake at different rates.

Allow to cool on the baking sheets for 5 minutes before transferring to a wire rack to cool completely.

Add 8 black candy melts to the white candy melts and melt together to make a gray color.

Dip the whole blade of the cookie knife (but not the handle) into the gray melted candy, allow any excess to drip off, and place on a sheet of parchment paper to set.

9   Once all blades are dipped, place the remaining gray melted candy into a piping bag fitted with a #1 plain tip.

10 Pipe a thin gray line close to the edge, around the outlines of the body cookies.

11 Once the blades are set, melt the remaining black candy melts and dip the handles of each of the knives so the black meets up with the gray and there is no cookie showing through. Use tweezers to place 3 dragées in a line up the handle of each knife (to look like rivets) and place on parchment paper to set.

12 Transfer the black melted candy to a zip-seal bag. Melt the red candy melts and place them into another zip-seal bag. Cut a small corner from the red bag and a slightly larger corner from the black bag.

One cookie at a time, use the black melted candy to flood the area inside the gray outline on the bodies. While the black is still wet, splatter some red melted candy droplets across the body to resemble blood and tap the cookie gently to even out the candy melts.

Drizzle and splatter red candy melt blood onto the tips and blades of the knives.

TIP: *If required, use a sharp knife to slice off any excess chocolate from around the cookie knives that may have pooled while setting.*

TIME SAVER: *Gingerdead Men CSI cookie cutters are available online if you want to save time on cutting the cookies.*

JUST MURDERE
MINI CAKES

MAKES 6 MINI

YOU'LL NEED

3 cups frozen raspberries
½ cup granulated sugar
¼ cup water
1 batch White Chocolate Mud Cake batter (page 210)
2½-inch round cookie cutter
1 batch Vanilla Bean Buttercream Frosting (page 215)
6 disposable "silver" plastic knives

1 In a saucepan, combine the raspberries, sugar, and water and cook over medium heat until thickened slightly but still pourable, 5 to 7 minutes.

2 Mash the mixture, pass through a sieve into a bowl to remove the seeds, and allow to cool.

3 Preheat the oven to 350°F. Grease and flour an 11½ x 15½-inch rimmed baking sheet. Line the bottom with parchment paper.

4 Make the cake batter and spread into the pan. Bake until the top of the cake springs back when touched, 25 to 30 minutes.

5 Allow the cake to cool in the pan for 15 minutes, then run a metal spatula around the edge of the pan and invert the cake onto a wire rack to cool completely.

6 Using the cookie cutter, cut out 18 rounds from the sheet cake.

7 Make the buttercream. Top a round of cake with a generous 1½ teaspoons of frosting and spread out to the edges. Add ½ teaspoon of raspberry sauce and stack another cake round on top. Repeat with more frosting and raspberry sauce and a third layer. Return the mini cakes to the fridge for 30 minutes to set.

8 Once set, frost the entire cake and use a ruler to smooth off the sides and even out the top.

9 Place 1 tablespoon of raspberry sauce on top of each cake and use the back of the spoon to push the sauce to the edges, allowing it to spill over, creating a "dripping blood" effect.

10 Stab a plastic knife into the center of each cake at a slight angle and drizzle a little more raspberry "blood" down the blade.

MONEY SAVER: *Save the cake scraps for making cake pop dough.*

SLIME-FILLED SPIDERS

MAKES 10 SPIDERS

YOU'LL NEED

9 ounces black candy melts
Red sprinkles
10 Whoppers or malt balls
10 black licorice wheels
1 box (3 ounces) lime Jell-O
½ cup boiling water
4 large ice cubes
2 tablespoons sweetened condensed milk

1 Melt the black candy melts (see page 220) and place a teaspoon of melted candy into each of 20 cavities of a cake pop mold (or the cavities of a 1½-inch sphere chocolate mold), spreading up the sides. Refrigerate to set.

2 Apply an additional teaspoon of candy melts and again spread up the sides to make a double coat. Refrigerate to set.

3 Spread the sprinkles on a small plate or bowl. Dip each Whopper into the melted candy just enough to create a ¼-inch-diameter round, then immediately dip into the sprinkles.

4 Make 8 legs for each spider: Unfurl the licorice wheels and cut each into 3-inch lengths and then cut each of those lengthwise into ⅛-inch-wide "legs." Cut 2 small triangles per spider to make small fangs.

5 Once set, release the black shells from the cake pop mold, then return them to the mold.

6 In a heatproof bowl, stir the Jell-O mix and boiling water until dissolved. Add the ice cubes to cool rapidly and then stir in the condensed milk.

7 Fill the black shells in the cake pop mold with the cooled Jell-O mixture and place in the fridge until completely set.

8 Remove the filled shells from the mold.

9 Heat a small skillet over medium heat. Touch the rim of one half of a black shell onto the surface of the pan for 5 seconds. Immediately use the melted edge to stick to the unmelted edge of a second shell.

10 Repeat until all the shells are spheres full of Jell-O.

11 Place 1 tablespoon of melted candy onto a piece of parchment paper and center a Jell-O-filled sphere over the candy melts. Immediately place 4 spider legs on each side, evenly spaced and supported by a little rolled tissue or paper towel to keep them upright.

12 Once set, use a little more melted candy to affix the Whopper to the front of the spider and the fangs to the front of the Whopper.

TIP: *To personalize your spiders, decorate their backs with colored candy melt accents and sprinkles for "hair." Or change up the color of the black shells to resemble your most feared species.*

7 ounces dark chocolate candy melts

2 cups crushed chocolate sandwich cookies
(about 20, cream filling left in)

4 tablespoons (2 ounces) salted butter, melted

6 (½-pint) square jars with lids

35 ounces full-fat cream cheese, at room temperature

1⅔ cups (200g) powdered sugar

2 teaspoons vanilla extract

½ teaspoon green food color paste

3 cups heavy cream, lightly whipped to soft peaks

12 brown M&M's

1 Melt the candy melts (see page 220) and place in a zip-seal bag. Cut off a very small corner.

2 Pipe small solid triangles onto a sheet of parchment paper. They don't need to be even and can vary a little in size. You'll need about 12 per jar, for a total of 72. Refrigerate to set.

3 In a bowl, combine the cookie crumbs and butter and mix well. Place 2 tablespoons loosely into the bottom of each jar.

4 Take the set triangles and place 3 per side around the outside of the cookie crumbs with the flat sides pressed up against the inside of the jar (this is Frankenstein's "hair").

FRANKENSTEIN CHEESECAKES

MAKES 6 SERVINGS

5 Once the triangles are in place, compact the cookie crumb mixture using the back of a spoon; it will help to hold the chocolate shards firmly in place. Refrigerate.

6 In a mixer bowl, beat the cream cheese, powdered sugar, and vanilla until whipped. Add the food color paste and mix thoroughly, tinting the mixture a little darker than you want the final product to be. Fold in the whipped cream, which will lighten the color of the mixture.

7 Spoon the cheesecake mixture into a piping bag and cut the end to make a ¾-inch opening. Pipe the mixture into the jars, starting in the center and finishing ½ inch above the top of the jar.

8 Tap the jar gently on the counter and, if need be, use a spoon to compact the cheesecake mixture into the corners of the jar so no air pockets are visible, then use an offset spatula to smooth the top of the cheesecake so it's flush with the jar rim.

9 Add the lids and allow to set in the fridge for 2 hours.

10 Once set, turn the jar over so the lid is now the base.

11 Dry off any condensation from the jar and use a black marker to draw on Frankenstein's face and scars. Place a small dab of melted candy on the back of 2 M&M's and use it as a glue to attach them to opposite sides of the jar to make the bolts in Frankenstein's neck.

Witches' Cauldron PUNCH

MAKES 3 QUARTS

YOU'LL NEED

1 box (3 ounces) lime Jell-O

1 cup boiling water

4 cups cold water

4 cups pineapple juice, chilled

Large watertight cauldron (see Note)

Dry ice (available at ice supply stores)

1 pint vanilla ice cream

Green food coloring

1 liter lemon-lime soda (such as Sprite)

1 In a heatproof bowl, dissolve the Jell-O in the boiling water and stir until there are no crystals. Add the cold water to cool the mixture. Add the pineapple juice and refrigerate until ready to serve.

2 Just before serving, place a large punch bowl (at least 4-quart capacity) into the empty cauldron.

3 Place chunks of dry ice in the base of the cauldron, *not* in the punch bowl. Handle with gloves, as dry ice will burn the skin. Dry ice should not be consumed.

4 Pour the refrigerated mixture into the punch bowl, and place 6 large scoops of vanilla ice cream on top. Add a few drops of food coloring to the bottle of soda, then pour into the punch bowl a little at a time until the bowl reaches capacity.

5 Finally, add hot water to the base of the cauldron (in between the punch bowl and cauldron) and watch it smoke, boil, and bubble.

NOTE: *You need a cauldron large enough for the punch bowl to fit inside, and the rim of the punch bowl should line up with the rim of the cauldron. If necessary, use a smaller upturned bowl to prop it up.*

Eyeball MILKSHAKES

YOU'LL NEED

Strawberry sundae syrup
6 milkshake glasses
4½ cups whole milk
1 pint vanilla ice cream
1 scoop chocolate ice cream
1 cup heavy cream, whipped to stiff peaks
6 candy eyeballs

1 Pour ½ inch of strawberry sundae syrup into a shallow bowl.

2 Dip the rims of the glasses into the syrup, tilting slightly to allow excess drips to fall before turning upright and allowing the syrup to drip down the inside and the outside. Refrigerate the glasses.

3 In a blender, combine the milk, vanilla ice cream, and chocolate ice cream and blend until thick and smooth.

4 Pour into the chilled glasses. Put the whipped cream in a piping bag fitted with a star tip and pipe whipped cream on top. Add some streaks of strawberry syrup, and finish with a candy eyeball.

TIME SAVER: *You can edge the glasses in advance, which also helps the blood drips to stay in place when you add the milkshake.*

BLEEDING CANDLES

YOU'LL NEED

White and black pillar candles

Red candles or sealing wax

GET CRAFTY

1   Use a warmed spoon to scrape out a portion in the center of each pillar candle. Make it about 1 inch deep, but leave ½ inch around the outside edges.

2   Place the pillar candles onto a sheet of parchment paper.

3   Light the red candle or sealing wax and allow the wax to dribble onto the pillar candles, pooling a little in the center, dripping over the edges, and eventually pooling a little at the bottom.

4   Trim the wick so it's not more than ½ inch long.

TIP: *You can make these using battery-operated candles for a longer-lasting, kid-safe option.*

MUMMY DRINKING JARS

Makes 6

TIP: *These also make great candle holders.*

YOU'LL NEED

6 (1-pint) mason jars
Gold spray paint
12 large googly eyes (self-adhesive are best)
3 rolls white gauze bandages
Tape

GET CRAFTY

1 Once you assemble your materials **A**, arrange the mason jars upside down on a flat surface so no paint can enter the jar and spray with gold spray paint. Allow to dry.

2 Place 2 googly eyes on the top third of the jars and stick in place **B**.

3 Affix one end of a bandage at the base of the jar using a little tape. Wind the gauze all the way around the jar until it's covered in a mummylike wrap allowing the gold to peek through between the gauze and leaving a good peek-through around the eyes **C**. Secure the gauze at the back with a little more tape.

A MOST
FRIGHTENING PARTY

I went for lots of black with green accents and a touch of gold—steering away from too much orange—to give this party a creepily classy edge.

Because the hutch is so tall, I was able to create a monumental dessert display without taking up too much space in my room, which allowed more space for other horrifying elements.

A MOST
FRIGHTENING
PARTY

I STYLED THIS PARTY in an old hutch. I bought a secondhand wooden hutch online for a song and painted it black—just a really rough coat. I know it seems like extra work to buy a piece of furniture, but for fifty dollars and a few fake spiderwebs I got a table, a backdrop, and a useful piece of furniture I can style up for the next event! As an added bonus, I kept all the cutlery and utensils for the party in the drawers and candy items in the cupboard for easy access to top up my dessert display during the party.

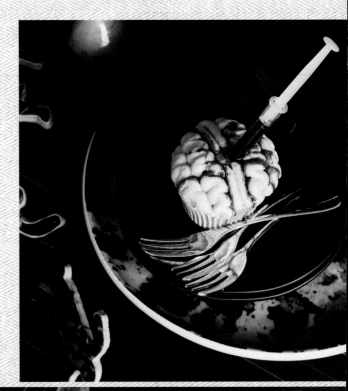

There aren't too many occasions for making food look quite as scary as Halloween, and I eagerly anticipate the season every year. My kids are just as excited, and they love nothing more than to eat a spider or devour zombie brains.

Although I must confess to loving all things pretty pink and a little bit colorful, I get so excited at the idea of "breaking the baking rules" at Halloween—the more gruesome the better, and absolutely anything goes!

RUSTIC
ROMANCE

TREE
STUMP
CAKE

MAKES ONE 7-LAYER CAKE

2 batches Rich Chocolate Mud Cake
    batter (page 211)

2 batches Milk Chocolate Ganache
    (page 219), whipped

1 cup granulated sugar

1 cup water

10-inch cake board

5-inch thin cake board

1 pound dark chocolate candy melts

6 graham cracker sheets

Dark green food coloring

Floral foam

4-inch thin cake board

Flowers

1 Preheat the oven to 325°F. Grease and flour four 6 x 3-inch round cake pans. Line the bottoms with rounds of parchment paper. (If you only have 2 pans, do this in batches, and do not mix up the second batch of batter until you're ready to bake the second set of cakes.)

2 Make the cake batter, scrape into the pans, and bake until a skewer inserted into the center comes out clean, about 1¼ hours. Let the cakes cool in the pans for 15 minutes, then invert onto a wire rack to cool completely.

3 While the cakes are cooling, make the ganache.

4 In a small saucepan, make a simple syrup. Bring the sugar and water to a boil, stirring until the sugar dissolves. Set aside.

5 Carve and level the cakes (see page 222, step 1). Halve each cake horizontally to make 8 layers; set one layer aside to use for tree "roots." Using the 10-inch cake board, stack and layer the remaining 7 layers, brushing each with simple syrup and frosting with ganache; using the 5-inch cake board, add supports at the fourth layer (see pages 222–23, steps 2, 3, and 4). Refrigerate for 30 minutes.

6 Apply a thin coat of ganache around the outside and top of the cake. Cut the reserved cake layer into 6 wedges like a pie. Trim the wedges to make 6 triangles and place them pointy side out around the base of the cake to create "roots." Carve the roots to blend them with the cake. Cover the roots with ganache and return to the fridge to chill for 20 minutes.

7 Melt the candy melts (see page 220).

8 Tear off three 9 x 13-inch pieces of parchment. Crumple each piece into a ball and then smooth out on the counter. This will provide texture.

9 Using an offset spatula, spread a thin layer of chocolate to coat Ⓐ. Roll up to form a 1-inch tube and refrigerate to set. Repeat to make a second tube.

10 Meanwhile, remove the cake from the fridge and apply a ¼-inch coating of ganache to the top and sides, and over the roots. Use a ruler to smooth out the top and roughly level off the sides.

11 Take the back of a teaspoon and drag the tip in a circular motion around the top of the cake to create circular "tree rings." Drag a fork up the side of the cake and over the roots to create texture.

12 Remove the chocolate tubes from the fridge and unroll.

13 Place pieces of the bark all over the cake, allowing them to just slightly protrude over the top of the cake Ⓑ, and get them as close together as possible. Use smaller pieces to cover the roots.

14 Remelt the rest of the candy melts along with any unused shards and, using a paintbrush, paint over the shards on the cake to join the chocolate pieces and create more texture Ⓒ.

15 Finely crush the graham crackers in a zip-seal bag. Add 1 teaspoon of food coloring and shake the bag to distribute. The crumbs should stick together a little and resemble moss. Stick small tufts of "moss" in patches around the base of the tree stump using the ganache as the "glue" Ⓓ.

16 Cut a small piece of floral foam and place onto the 4-inch cake board. Cover in plastic wrap to prevent the foam from touching the cake. Insert flowers into the plastic-covered floral foam. Place onto the top of the cake, securing with a little leftover ganache if required.

TIP: *This is a beautiful wedding or engagement cake, but replacing the fresh flowers with some small, brightly colored edible blooms and tiny fairies makes a beautiful woodland fairy cake for kids.*

FLOWERPOT CUPCAKES

MAKES 24 CUPCAKES

YOU'LL NEED

24 Classic Chocolate Cupcakes
  (page 209)
24 small terra-cotta pots
7 ounces dark chocolate candy melts
½ cup heavy cream
1 cup crushed chocolate sandwich cookies
  (about 10, cream filling left in)
24 green straws
24 thin-stemmed fresh flowers

1 Bake and cool the cupcakes as directed.

2 Place each cupcake in a small terra-cotta pot.

3 Combine the candy melts and heavy cream in a
   microwave-safe bowl and microwave in 30-second
   intervals, stirring in between until the candy melts
   have completely melted.

4 Spoon about 1 tablespoon of the chocolate
   mixture on top of each cupcake, ensuring the
   chocolate doesn't spill over the outsides of the
   pots. Sprinkle with crushed chocolate cookie "dirt."

5 Cut the straws to 4 inches each and insert one into
   the center of each cupcake. Place a single flower in
   each straw vase.

Chocolate-Filled
PUMPKINS

MAKES 12 PUMPKINS

1 batch Classic Vanilla Cake batter (page 208)
Orange food color paste
½ batch White Chocolate Ganache (page 219)
2 cups chocolate hazelnut spread
6 cinnamon sticks, cut into 1-inch lengths

1   Preheat the oven to 350°F. Grease and flour two 12-cavity mini Bundt cake pans. (Or bake in two batches.)

2   Make the cake batter and fold in 1 teaspoon of food coloring. Divide the batter among the Bundt cake cups, filling them three-fourths full. Bake until the tops spring back when touched, 12 to 15 minutes. Let cool in the pan for 15 minutes before turning out onto a wire rack. Chill in the freezer for 20 minutes or until firm.

3   Make the ganache. Measure out ½ cup and stir in ¼ teaspoon food coloring. Leave the remain-der white.

4   Once the cakes are firm, use a serrated knife to level each mini Bundt so the bottoms are flat.

5   Place the cakes back into the pan for stability and use a teaspoon to dig out a ¼-inch-deep trench all around the center hole, leaving ¼ inch of cake on both sides. Repeat for all the cakes.

6   Place the chocolate hazelnut spread into a zip-seal bag and cut off a small corner. Pipe the spread into the trench to just below level with the cake.

7   Place the orange ganache mixture into a zip-seal bag, snip off a corner, and pipe a thin line along the outer and inner rims of the cakes. Pair up the cakes, turning one upside down and placing it on top of the other, to glue together. Refrigerate for 15 minutes to set.

8   Place the white ganache into a zip-seal bag and cut off a small corner. Pipe the ganache over the cakes, starting in the center and allowing the ganache to drip down the sides. Place a piece of cinnamon stick in the center of each cake to be the stem.

Under the Apple Tree

LAYERED CAKES

MAKES 12 SERVINGS

1 batch White Chocolate Mud Cake batter (page 210)

2-inch round cookie cutter

12 (½-pint) mason jars

APPLES:

1½ pounds green apples, such as Granny Smith

1 teaspoon ground cinnamon

2½ tablespoons packed light brown sugar

2½ tablespoons water

CRUMBLE:

2 cups rolled oats

1 cup all-purpose flour

½ cup packed light brown sugar

1¾ sticks (7 ounces) salted butter, melted

TREE:

9 ounces brown candy melts

Apple Treetop template (page 226)

12 jumbo wooden craft sticks (6 x ¾ inch)

9 ounces green candy melts

About 84 red M&M's Minis

1 Preheat the oven to 325°F. Grease and flour an 11½ x 15½-inch rimmed baking sheet. Line the bottom with parchment paper.

2 Make the cake batter and scrape it into the pan. Bake until the center springs back when touched, 25 to 30 minutes. (Leave the oven on and increase the oven temperature to 350°F.)

3 Allow the cake to cool in the pan for 15 minutes and then transfer to a wire rack to cool completely.

4 **Prepare the apples:** Peel, core, and dice the apples. Place in a small saucepan along with the cinnamon, brown sugar, and water and cook over medium heat until the water has evaporated and the apples have softened with a golden glow.

5 **Make the crumble:** Line a rimmed baking sheet with parchment. In a medium bowl, combine the oats, flour, brown sugar, and butter and stir well. Spread out on the baking sheet and bake until golden brown, about 20 minutes.

6 Take the cookie cutter and cut 24 rounds from the cake. Place a round of cake in the bottom of each jar, followed by 1 tablespoon of apple mixture and 1 tablespoon of crumble. Repeat with a second layer of cake, apple, and crumble. (You'll have plenty of crumble left.)

7 Melt the brown candy melts (see page 220) in a deep container and dip the craft sticks three-quarters of the way into the melted candy. Place onto parchment to set.

8 **Make the tree:** Trace the outline of the Apple Treetop template onto a piece of parchment.

9 Melt the green candy melts and place in a zip-seal bag. Place a craft stick so it's slightly overlapping the bottom of the treetop template. Pipe an outline around the treetop (going over the craft stick as you do), then fill in with small swirls to resemble leaves. Before the green melted candy sets, place a few red M&M's "apples" on each tree.

10 Make a slit down through the center of the top cake layer in the jar. Carefully drive the craft stick into the slit so half the "trunk" protrudes above the top of the cake.

11 Add a little more crumble around the tree base.

> **TIME SAVER:** *You can make the trees, cook the apples, and bake the crumble up to two days before using. Store the apples in the fridge and the rest at room temperature.*

Pumpkin Spice
LATTE PARFAITS

MAKES 6 SERVINGS

YOU'LL NEED

2 cups finely crushed gingersnaps (about 9 ounces), the texture of fine sand

4 tablespoons salted butter, melted

6 (8-ounce) latte glasses

½ cup packed light brown sugar

½ cup boiling water

8 ounces cream cheese, at room temperature

1½ cups canned unsweetened pumpkin puree

½ teaspoon vanilla extract

½ teaspoon ground cinnamon

⅛ teaspoon ground cloves

⅛ teaspoon ground ginger

Pinch of ground nutmeg

2½ cups heavy cream

Caramel topping, for serving

1 In a bowl, stir the gingersnap crumbs and butter. Spoon about ¼ cup into the bottom of each glass and compact with the back of a spoon.

2 In a small heatproof bowl, combine the brown sugar and boiling water and allow to sit for 15 minutes until the sugar dissolves.

3 In a mixer bowl, combine the cream cheese, pumpkin puree, vanilla, cinnamon, cloves, ginger, and nutmeg and beat on high speed until light and fluffy. Gradually add the brown sugar liquid and mix well.

4 In a separate bowl, whip 2 cups of the heavy cream on high speed until soft peaks just start to form.

5 Fold the whipped cream into the pumpkin mixture using large, sweeping motions until the cheesecake mixture is well combined.

6 Place the mixture into a piping bag and cut a ½-inch opening from the end. Pipe an even amount of cheesecake mixture into each glass and place in the fridge to set.

7 Whip the remaining ½ cup heavy cream to stiff peaks. Place a tablespoon of whipped cream on top of each glass and use the back of a knife to smooth the cream to a flat surface to resemble latte foam.

8 Drizzle with caramel topping and serve with a long spoon.

GIANT PEANUT BUTTER CUP

MAKES ONE 9-INCH TART

26 ounces milk chocolate (compound or tempered, see Note, page 221)
2⅓ cups (21 ounces) smooth peanut butter
5 cups (600g) powdered sugar, sifted
1 stick plus 1 tablespoon (4½ ounces) salted butter, melted

1 Grease the bottom of a nonstick 9-inch fluted tart pan (with a removable bottom) with butter or oil and line with a round of parchment paper.

2 Melt 16 ounces of the chocolate to a smooth pourable consistency. Pour the chocolate into the bottom of the tart pan, spreading up the sides using a spoon. This should be quite thick and spread evenly over the whole tart pan. Refrigerate for 15 minutes to set.

3 In a large mixer bowl, beat the peanut butter, powdered sugar, and butter. The mixture should be well mixed but a little firm and lumpy.

4 Remove the chocolate shell from the pan and set aside.

5 Scrape the peanut butter filling into the empty tart pan and press firmly until you have a compressed even disk of peanut butter filling. Cut away a ¼-inch border from the outside edges of the peanut butter disk using a knife. Then slide an offset spatula under the filling to release it from the base and transfer it. It will behave a little like pizza dough as you transfer it to the chocolate shell. It should sit just below the edge of the shell.

6 Return the entire peanut butter cup to the tart pan (make sure it's clean).

7 Melt the remaining 10 ounces of chocolate and pour onto the top of the peanut butter cup. Use a ruler to even out the top of the peanut butter cup and make it perfectly flat and smooth. Refrigerate for 15 minutes.

8 Store and serve at room temperature. Cut with a hot knife to avoid cracking.

SPICED ORANGE ICED TEA

MAKES 2 QUARTS

YOU'LL NEED

¼ cup granulated sugar

1½ cups boiling water

5 regular black tea bags

6 cinnamon sticks

1 orange, sliced crosswise
into rounds and seeded

4 cups ice, plus more for
serving

6 cups cold water

1 cup blood orange juice

Orange wedges

1 In a heatproof bowl, dissolve the sugar
in ½ cup of the boiling water.

2 In a separate bowl, steep the tea bags
and cinnamon sticks in the remaining
1 cup boiling water for 20 minutes.
Remove the tea bags and leave the
cinnamon sticks to infuse.

3 Just before serving, remove the
cinnamon sticks. Place the orange
slices into a 3½-quart drink dispenser,
followed by the ice. Pour in the cold
water, cooled tea mixture, blood orange
juice, and dissolved sugar and stir well.

4 Garnish 10 small glasses with orange
wedges and allow the guests to serve
themselves from the drink dispenser.

S'MORES HOT CHOCOLATE

MAKES 6 SERVINGS

YOU'LL NEED

1 tablespoon honey or light corn syrup

6 (8-ounce) mugs

½ cup crushed graham cracker crumbs

6 cups whole milk

8 ounces dark chocolate, chopped

12 to 18 regular marshmallows

1. Position a rack near the top of the oven and preheat the broiler. Line a baking sheet with parchment paper.

2. Rub a little honey around the top edges of the mugs, including the rims and about ½ inch down the sides. Place the graham cracker crumbs in a shallow bowl. Dip the mugs into the graham cracker crumbs to coat in a thick coating.

3. In a saucepan, bring the milk to a boil. Remove from the heat and whisk in the chocolate until it's completely melted. Divide evenly among the mugs, leaving ½ inch from the top of the rim.

4. Arrange the marshmallows on the baking sheet and broil until they just start to puff up and turn golden brown, 3 to 5 minutes.

5. Remove from the oven and use tongs to place 2 or 3 marshmallows on top of each hot chocolate.

TIP: *If you have a small blowtorch, you can place the marshmallows on top of the hot chocolate and brown with the torch.*

LACE DOILY
BUNTING

*Makes one
2½-yard length*

YOU'LL NEED

- 3 to 4 yards ribbon
- About 15 assorted lace doilies (different sizes, if possible)
- Mini clothespins
- Fabric glue (optional)

GET CRAFTY

1 Lay out the ribbon and evenly distribute the doilies along it, folding each in half over the ribbon.

2 Once you're happy with the placement, use mini clothespins to secure your bunting in place. For a more permanent result, affix the doilies to the ribbon with fabric glue before adding the clothespins.

CAKE TOPPER

Makes 1

YOU'LL NEED

8½ x 11-inch sheet of paper

A length of 16- or 18-gauge wire about 10 times longer than your printed word

Needle-nose pliers

Floral tape

GET CRAFTY

1 Start by writing out the word you want to use on the sheet of paper A.

2 Mark a starting point 12 inches in from the end of the wire and then begin bending and twisting the wire to follow the outline of the word you printed out. Use the needle-nose pliers each time there is a sharp turn or prominent curve in the lettering B.

3 Leave 12 inches at the end of the last letter before trimming the wire.

4 Use the needle-nose pliers to sharply turn the wire downward at the start and end of the word to create 2 long vertical supports for the topper.

5 Wrap a little floral tape around the base of each support to create a barrier between the metal and the cake C. The tape should cover any part of the wire intended to go inside the cake.

The late afternoon is a glorious time for a rustic affair. The light, colors, and softly setting sun enhance the beauty and add to the ambience.

The recipes, flavors, and DIY ideas for this party are all designed to highlight not only the fall season but the idea of embracing the rawness of natural textures, earthy colors, and spiced fragrant undertones.

RUSTIC
PARTY

THIS PARTY is a total contradiction—rustic and raw meets soft lace and dainty desserts. I rented two huge wine barrels and laid a plank of raw wood across them, then used a light linen table runner and the softest pale pink and white flowers I could find. Empty photo frames hung from an old tree, stacked apple crates made up my backdrop, and bright orange accents added a pop of color and the feeling of fall.

A vintage affair is all about warm rustic tones and intimate settings, and it's the perfect excuse to go overboard with twinkling lights. Hang them from the trees, wind them through the desserts, string them around vases and candy jars, or add them to mason jars. When the sun starts to set, these tiny lights will shine their soft glow on the party and make the atmosphere magical.

Rustic weddings, barn locations, and raw, rough textures mixed with soft, dainty lace have become incredibly popular in recent times, and this chapter is all about the old, the new, and the beautifully distressed.

HAPPY
HOLIDAYS

CHAPTER №

8

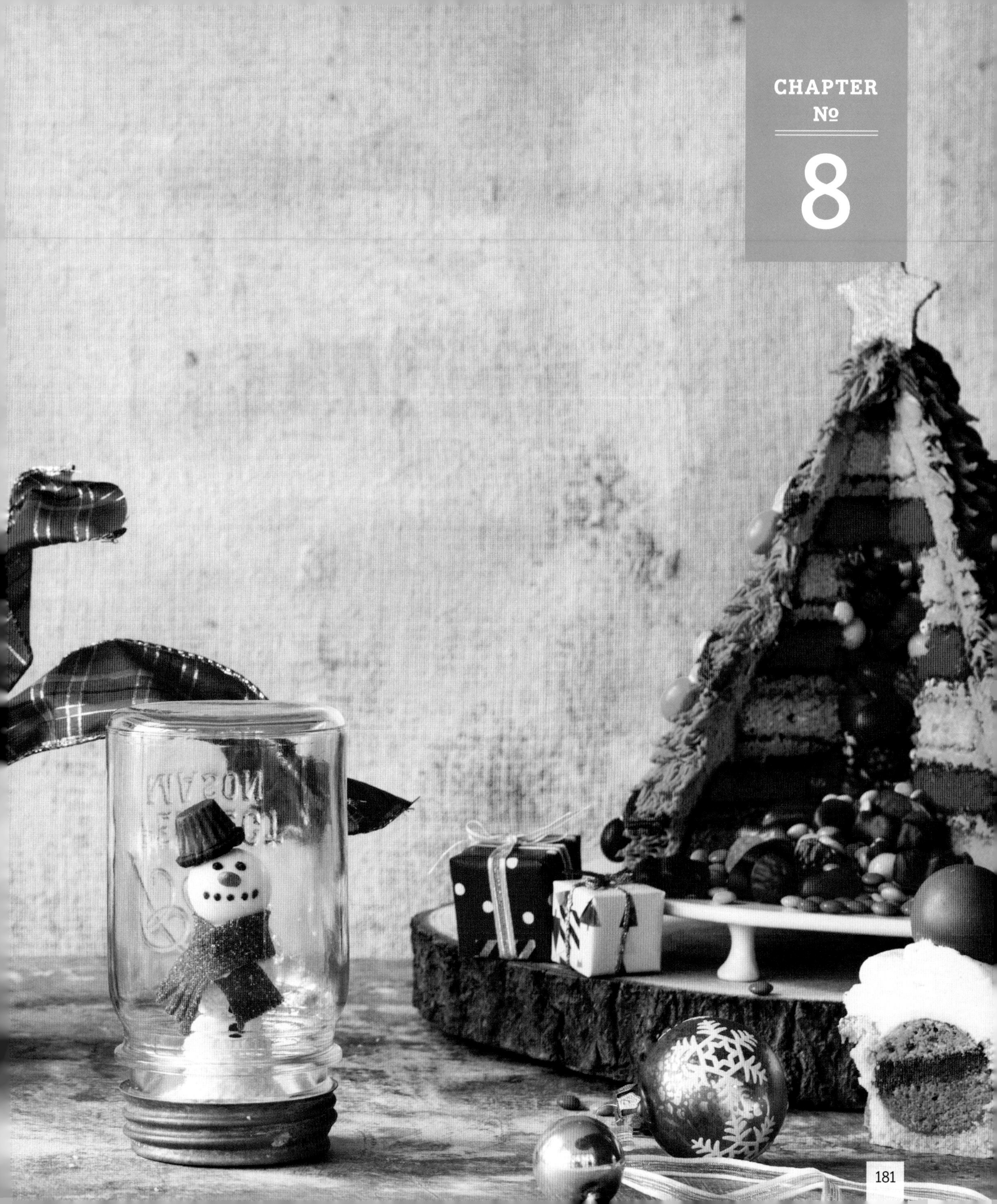

Christmas Tree
SURPRISE
CAKE

MAKES 1 CHRISTMAS TREE

3 batches Classic Vanilla Cake batter (page 208)

Red and green food coloring

2-inch round cookie cutter

3 batches Vanilla Bean Buttercream Frosting (page 215)

8-inch cake board

About 3 cups assorted candies

5 ounces white candy melts

About 20 colored Tic Tac candies

About 40 peanut M&M's

Small star cookie cutter

1 lollipop stick or skewer

Gold sanding sugar

1 Preheat the oven to 350°F. Grease and flour a 9 x 13-inch cake pan. Line the bottom with parchment paper.

2 You have to bake 3 cakes, but bake them one at a time, mixing up the batter only when you're ready to bake. For 2 of the cakes, tint the batter green. For the third cake, tint the batter red. Bake each cake until the center springs back when lightly touched, about 45 minutes.

3 Let the cake cool in the pan for 15 minutes, then invert the cake onto a wire rack to cool. Chill in the fridge for 30 minutes so the cake becomes firm.

4 Carve and level the cakes (see page 222, step 1).

5 Using plates, bowls, glasses, or round cookie cutters to trace around, cut the following: From the two green cakes, cut out 4 rounds: 8-inch, 6-inch, 4-inch, and 2-inch. Then from the red cake, cut out 4 rounds: 7-inch, 5-inch, 3-inch, and 1-inch. Take the round cookie cutter and cut a hole through the centers of the 4-inch, 5-inch, 6-inch, and 7-inch layers. (Save all the scraps for making Christmas-colored cake pop dough!)

6 Make the buttercream frosting. Measure out 1 cup and tint it red. Tint the rest dark green.

7 Spread a little green frosting on the cake board, lay down the 8-inch green cake layer, and spread a layer of frosting on top.

8 Add the 7-inch red layer and repeat, taking care not to frost the inside edges of the center hole. Continue stacking and frosting gradually smaller cake layers until you reach the 4-inch layer.

9 Take the 3 cups of candy and fill the center core of the tree A , pressing down a little to compact the candy. Frost the top of the 4-inch layer and continue stacking and frosting until all the layers are stacked.

10 Once stacked, take a serrated knife and gently carve away the sharp edges of the layers to form a tall cone shape. Apply a very thin "crumb coat" of frosting all over the outside of the cake B . Set in the fridge for 30 minutes.

11 Meanwhile, make the Christmas lights. Melt the candy melts (see page 220). Cut the colored Tic Tacs in half crosswise. Use a toothpick dipped in the melted candy to attach a Tic Tac to the end of a peanut M&M of the same color (the M&M is the bulb and the Tic Tac is the base). You will need about 40 of these.

12 To make the star for the top of the tree, trace around a star cookie cutter onto parchment. Pipe an outline of white melted candy, then fill in the shape. Place a lollipop stick in the center and cover with more melted candy. Sprinkle with sanding sugar and let set at room temperature.

13 Place the green frosting into a piping bag fitted with a #21 open star tip. Starting at the top of the cake, pipe ¾-inch-long strands of frosting in neat rows around the entire cake, like layers of pine branches on a Christmas tree C .

14 Once the cake is covered, place the red frosting into a piping bag fitted with a #21 piping tip and pipe draping lines of "tinsel" around the cake. Attach the colored M&M lights directly to the red frosting D . Work quickly here, as the frosting will start to form a crust, which can make attaching the decorations difficult.

15 Take the star and flip it over. Coat the back with white melted candy and sprinkle with sanding sugar. Allow to set. Insert the lollipop stick into the center of the top of the tree.

> **TIME SAVER:** *Make the lights and star ahead and store in a container at room temperature for up to 2 weeks.*

Stuffed Stocking
SURPRISE COOKIES

MAKES 8 COOKIES

1 batch Vanilla Sugar Cookie dough (page 214), plus flour for rolling out

1 tablespoon red food color paste

Christmas Stocking template (page 227)

7 ounces white candy melts

Tiny red and green festive candies, such as Nerds, M&M's Minis, or sprinkles

1 Make the cookie dough, adding the food color paste when you add the vanilla. Split into 2 portions and refrigerate for 30 minutes.

2 Preheat the oven to 350°F. Line the baking sheets with parchment paper.

3 Trace the outline of the Christmas Stocking and then cut it out of thick card stock to use as a template. (Cut out the central rectangle as well.)

4 Working with one portion of dough at a time, on a floured surface, roll the dough ¼ inch thick. Use the template to cut out stockings, rerolling the scraps to cut out as many as you can. You need multiples of 3, as each "surprise cookie" is made up of a set of 3 cookies.

5 Arrange the cookies on baking sheets, but have one cookie out of every set of cookies inverted (toe pointing the opposite way). Use the rectangle part of the template to cut a hole out of every third cookie. Bake until you just start to see the cookies darkening around the edges, 10 to 12 minutes. Let cool for 10 minutes on the pan, then transfer to a wire rack.

6 Grate ¼ cup of candy melts using a fine grater and set aside.

7 Melt the remaining candy melts (see page 220) and place into a zip-seal bag, cutting a small tip off the corner.

8 Assemble the stocking sets so each has a front, a middle, and a back stocking, with the "baked side" of the front and back stockings facing inward.

9 Pipe a thin line of melted candy close to the edge of the "baked side" of the back stocking and then take a middle stocking and place it on top.

10 Fill the stocking cavity with the candies. Do not overfill.

11 Pipe a line of melted candy on top of the middle stocking and place the final whole stocking on top, baked side in. Pipe around the toe, heel, and top of the top stocking and immediately sprinkle with the grated candy melts to create a fluffy effect.

TIP: *Use a spoon to sprinkle on the grated melts so you don't crush them or melt them with your fingers.*

Christmas Candle
PUSH POPS

MAKES 12 PUSH POPS

1 batch White Chocolate Mud Cake batter (page 210)

12 push pop containers

5 large candy canes

1 batch Vanilla Bean Buttercream Frosting (page 215)

7 ounces white candy melts

12 white birthday candles

1 Preheat the oven to 350°F. Grease and flour an 11½ x 15½-inch rimmed baking sheet. Line the bottom with parchment paper.

2 Make the batter and spread into the baking sheet. Bake until the top of the cake springs back when touched, 25 to 30 minutes.

3 Allow the cake to cool in the pan for 15 minutes, then transfer to the fridge for another 30 minutes until it's just chilled.

4 Take an empty push pop container and use it as a guide to cut 36 rounds from the chilled cake using a sharp knife (save the scraps for making cake pop dough).

5 Place the candy canes in a zip-seal plastic bag and use a rolling pin to crush them into small chunks. Make the frosting, folding in the crushed candy canes at the end. Transfer to a piping bag and cut off a ½-inch tip.

6 Place a round of cake into the base of each push pop container, followed by a swirl of frosting, then another cake round and another frosting swirl. Insert a third cake round, top with frosting, and use a knife to smooth and level the frosting to a flat top.

7 Melt the candy melts (see page 220).

8 Place 2 teaspoons of melted candy onto the top of the frosting and use the back of the spoon to gently push the melted candy over the side to create wax drips. Immediately insert a birthday candle into the top of each push pop (see Tip).

TIP: *Don't light the candles until you're ready to serve, as they'll burn fairly quickly. For a longer-lasting candle, take a small tealight candle, activate the light, dip the base in melted candy melt, and allow to set (this prevents the nonedible elements from touching the edible ones). Place on top of each push pop in place of the birthday candles.*

HIDDEN ORNAMENT
CUPCAKES

MAKES 12 CUPCAKES

YOU'LL NEED

1 batch Classic Vanilla Cake batter (page 208)
Red and green food color pastes
2 ounces white candy melts
24 mini peanut butter cups (½ inch diameter)
Long yellow sprinkles
Large gumballs (1½ inch diameter)
1 batch Vanilla Bean Buttercream Frosting (page 215)

1 Preheat the oven to 350°F. Coat the 24 cavities of a 12-pop nonstick cake pop mold (top and bottom sections) with cooking spray.

2 Make the cake batter. Measure out half the batter and set aside. Divide the remaining batter evenly between 2 bowls. Color one bowl red and the other green.

3 Fill 6 cavities of the bottom section of the cake pop mold with the green batter and fill the remaining 6 cavities with the red batter. Each cake pop cavity should be filled to just over full.

4 Close the mold and bake until the mixture stops pushing out the breathing holes of the cake pop mold, 10 to 14 minutes. Check first at 10 minutes, and then every minute thereafter. Remove the baked balls from the mold and place in the freezer for 20 minutes.

5 Once cooled and semifrozen, use a serrated knife to cut a ¼-inch-thick slice from the center of each ball, leaving you with 2 hemispheres and the ¼-inch-thick disk. Reassemble the balls, matching the colors of the hemispheres, but replacing the center slice with the opposite color.

6 Melt the candy melts (see page 220) and place ¼ teaspoon onto either side of each middle disk. Attach a hemisphere to each side to create a completed ornament.

7 Line 12 cups of a muffin tin with paper liners.

8 Place 1 teaspoon of the reserved cake batter into the bottom of each of the cupcake liners. Place an ornament into the center of each liner and press down to secure, making sure the middle disk is horizontal and level.

9 Place the rest of the batter into a piping bag with no tip and pipe the batter first onto the top of the ornament to add weight and then around the outside of the ornament until the liner is three-fourths full.

10 Bake until the sides of the cupcake spring back when lightly touched, 13 to 16 minutes. Immediately transfer to a wire rack to cool.

11 Meanwhile, make the mini ornaments: Use a toothpick to make a small hole in the base of each mini peanut butter cup, dip a long sprinkle into a little melted candy, and insert into the hole (this is the ornament handle). Take the gumballs and use a little more melted candy to attach a peanut butter cup to each gumball.

12 Make the frosting and transfer to a piping bag fitted with a plain tip. Pipe a high frosting swirl and top each cupcake with a mini ornament.

A surprise baked right inside a cupcake is like a present within a present! (For the recipe, see page 191.)

NO BAKE

Glowing CANDY COTTAGE

MAKES 1 COTTAGE

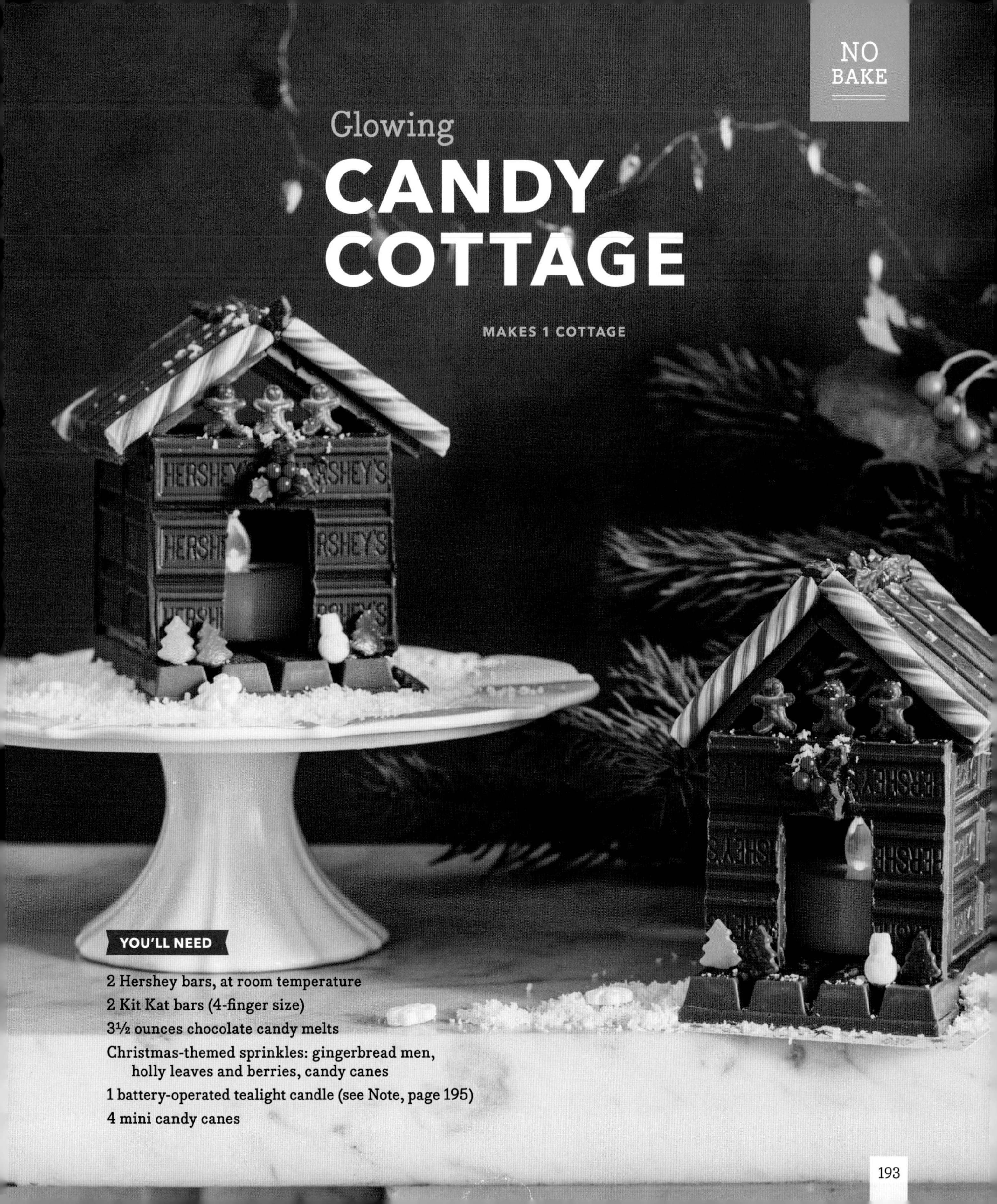

YOU'LL NEED

- 2 Hershey bars, at room temperature
- 2 Kit Kat bars (4-finger size)
- 3½ ounces chocolate candy melts
- Christmas-themed sprinkles: gingerbread men, holly leaves and berries, candy canes
- 1 battery-operated tealight candle (see Note, page 195)
- 4 mini candy canes

The kids and I make these every year and create an entire candy house village that shines through until Christmas. If any candles go out before, I tell them Santa snuck in and turned off the lights!

1 Warm a sharp knife in hot water before cutting 4 pieces, each 2 x 2⅜ inches, out of the Hershey bars (just under half a bar each). From one piece, cut out a door that is 1 x 1½ inches.

2 Cut one of the Kit Kat bars in half crosswise and set aside for making the roof. Refrigerate all the chocolate pieces for 15 minutes before proceeding.

3 Melt the candy melts (see page 220) and place in a zip-seal bag. Cut off a very small corner.

4 Position the whole Kit Kat bar so a narrow side is facing you. Pipe a line of melted candy down the long side of one of the Hershey pieces and stick it on top of the Kit Kat bar at the very back, with the chocolate "bricks" facing out.

5 Once set, take a second piece of Hershey and pipe a line of melted candy along the long side and up the short side. Place the Hershey piece on top of the Kit Kat bar along one side, meeting the back wall. Repeat with the third piece of Hershey on the opposite side. Pipe a line of melted candy along the front edge of both side walls and attach the front piece with the door cut out. Decorate the porch and above the door with sprinkles.

6 Activate the tea light candle and place inside the structure.

7 To make the roof, pipe a line of melted candy along the top edge of the two side walls and angle the Kit Kat pieces so the cut edges meet in the middle. Pipe a line of melted candy along the join of the Kit Kats and fill with holly and berry sprinkles. Snap the curved edges off 4 candy canes and use the melted candy to affix candy cane borders to the roofline, front, and back.

NOTE: *Before inserting the battery-operated candle in the candy cottage, make sure it has adequate battery life so that it will still be lit up at serving time.*

KIDS IN THE KITCHEN: *I make the basic shapes and let the kids decorate their own houses each year, resulting in a whole family village twinkling on the mantel on Christmas Eve.*

YOU'LL NEED

3½ ounces white candy melts

12 (1-pint) mason jars with lids

24 Raffaello coconut truffles (keep refrigerated until ready to use)

12 Lindt white chocolate truffles (keep refrigerated until ready to use)

2 ounces black candy melts

12 orange candy coated sunflower seeds

6 mini Oreos

6 mini peanut butter cups

Red candy straps

1 cup shredded coconut

1　Melt the white candy melts (see page 220) and place a tablespoon onto the inside of each of the jar lids. Set one coconut truffle into the white melted candy in each of the lids and refrigerate to set.

2　Once set, place ¼ teaspoon of white melted candy onto the coconut truffle and glue a second coconut truffle on top (for the snowman's body). Allow to set. Use more white melted candy to glue on a white chocolate truffle (the snowman's head) and allow to set.

Snowman
SNOW GLOBES

MAKES 12 SNOWMEN

3 Melt the black candy melts and use the flat end of a toothpick to fashion 2 black eyes and a line of black dots for a mouth. Place 3 black buttons down the front of the two bottom truffles.

4 Place a small dab of white melted candy on the fat side of a sunflower seed and attach it as the snowman's nose.

5 Split the mini Oreos and scrape the cream filling off the wafers.

6 Use a small amount of black melted candy to glue together a mini peanut butter cup and a mini Oreo to make a hat. Use white melted candy to attach the hat to the snowman's head.

7 Make the snowmen's scarves: Cut a candy strap into a piece 5 inches long and ¼ inch wide and use scissors to cut tassels on the ends. Wrap the scarf around the snowman's neck. Secure with a little white melted candy.

8 Sprinkle the base of the lid with a little coconut "snow" and carefully invert the jar over the snowman, screwing into the lid to create an edible snow globe.

HOT CHOCOLATE
Gingerbread Men

MAKES 6 SERVINGS

9 red buttons and 9 white buttons, about ½ inch

Craft glue

6 (10-ounce) heatproof milk bottles

1 yard (1-inch-wide) wired Christmas-themed ribbon

8 cups whole milk

2-inch piece fresh ginger

2 cinnamon sticks

14 ounces milk chocolate, chopped

2 ounces white candy melts

6 (2-inch-diameter) chocolate-coated cookies

12 Christmas-striped straws

1 Take 3 buttons of the same color and glue them in a line down the front of each of the milk bottles. You will end up with 3 bottles with white buttons and 3 with red.

2 Cut the ribbon into six 6-inch lengths and wrap a ribbon "scarf" around each bottle neck, securing with a loose knot.

3 In a saucepan, bring the milk, ginger, and cinnamon sticks to a simmer over medium heat. Remove from the heat, use a spoon to remove any milk skin, then add the milk chocolate, stirring until completely melted. Infuse for 15 to 20 minutes.

4 Melt the candy melts (see page 220) and place in a zip-seal bag. Snip off a small corner and pipe 2 small eyes and a mouth onto the front of each of the cookies.

5 Just before serving, bring the chocolate back to a simmer. Strain into a pitcher (discard the solids) and pour into the milk bottles.

6 Add 2 straws and place a small amount of melted candy on the back of the cookie, using it to "glue" the gingerbread "face" to the straws so the cookie rests snugly on the bottle rim and the straws hold it in place.

TIP: *You can chill this hot chocolate for a delicious refreshing milk drink in warmer climates.*

GRINCH-NOG

MAKES 6 SERVINGS

YOU'LL NEED

Red sprinkles

6 glass mugs

1 tablespoon light corn syrup or honey

1 quart whole milk

1½ cups granulated sugar

1 teaspoon vanilla extract

2 cinnamon sticks

1 teaspoon grated nutmeg

2 cups heavy cream

8 extra-large egg yolks

Green food coloring

Whipped cream, for serving

1 Fill a shallow dish with ½ inch of red sprinkles. Using your finger, rim the top ½ inch of each glass with a little corn syrup, and then dip into the red sprinkles to create a red sprinkle rim.

2 In a medium saucepan, combine the milk, sugar, vanilla, cinnamon sticks, and nutmeg and bring to a boil. Set aside to cool for 15 minutes.

3 Place the heavy cream and egg yolks into a large heatproof bowl and whisk for 1 minute. Remove the cinnamon sticks from the milk mixture and whisk 1 cup of the milk mixture into the heavy cream mixture.

4 Bring a medium pot of water to a rapid boil. Reduce to a simmer and place the bowl with the heavy cream mixture over the pot, making sure the water does not touch the bottom of the bowl. Whisking constantly, gradually add the remaining milk mixture until it has all been incorporated. Whisk until very warm to the touch (but not hot), light, frothy, and airy, about 5 minutes.

5 Add a few drops of food coloring to bring out the Grinch who stole Christmas, pour into the red-rimmed glasses, top with whipped cream and sprinkles, and serve.

FRAGRANT PLACE CARDS

Makes 1

YOU'LL NEED

1 cinnamon stick
Alphabet stamps
Ink pad
1 sprig rosemary
2 inches thin red ribbon

GET CRAFTY

1 Stamp a guest's name along the cinnamon stick using alphabet stamps.

2 Take the sprig of rosemary, join the two ends, and secure with the ribbon to make a tiny evergreen wreath. Tie the ends of the ribbon into a small bow.

3 Thread the cinnamon stick through the center of the rosemary wreath and place on a napkin for a fragrant, personalized place setting.

YOU'LL NEED

Advent Calendar template (page 227)

Card stock

1 (24-cup) mini muffin tin (try to find one with a small hole at one end)

Craft paper in assorted Christmas colors and patterns

Mini candy bars, treats, or gifts (small enough to fit in a mini muffin cup)

Small number stickers: 1 through 24

Double-sided tape

Ribbon

GET CRAFTY

1   Trace the Advent Calendar onto a piece of card stock and cut out to use as a template.

2   Using the template as a guide, cut out 24 assorted colored and patterned "covers" for the muffin tin cups **A**.

3   Place a treat in each muffin cup **B**.

4   Affix a number sticker to each muffin cup cover, and attach the covers using 4 small pieces of double-sided tape, placing the numbers randomly, not in sequence **C**.

5   If the muffin tin has a small hole, use this to hang the calendar with a ribbon.

Because Christmas is the time of year when I put the most thought into place settings, I decided to use parts of my dessert display to create extra-fun, delicious elements for each placement at the table.

My Christmas dining table doubled as the dessert display so my guests could ogle the delicious sweet treats throughout their meal and spend as much time admiring my desserts as I'd spent making them! Using the center aisle of the table allows enough space on either side for the meal to be served, but also provides a fun, vibrant, and festive display with a unique twist—everything's edible!

HOLIDAY
PARTY

I LOVE being in charge of desserts for the Christmas meal, because my job is generally done by Christmas Eve and I'm one of the few who doesn't need to make frequent trips to the kitchen on Christmas Day, so I can spend more time enjoying my loved ones.

Plus, Santa brings extra gifts for the person who makes his nighttime stocking piñata cookie and adorable gingerbread man hot chocolate . . . right?

I also added an edible candle push pop display, which shines from the mantel with a warm Christmas glow.

Christmas is all about connecting with people and sharing a day that comes only once a year, and for my family, it's all about the kids. Well, the kids and the dessert.

THE
BASICS

CLASSIC VANILLA CAKE & CUPCAKES

*Makes one 8 x 3-inch-high cake
or 24 cupcakes*

YOU'LL NEED

2 sticks plus 2 tablespoons
    (9 ounces) salted butter,
    at room temperature

1 cup plus 3 tablespoons
    (225g) superfine sugar

3 extra-large eggs, at room
    temperature

½ vanilla bean (halved crosswise),
    split lengthwise, or 1 teaspoon
    vanilla extract

3 tablespoons vegetable oil

2 cups (260g) all-purpose flour

1 tablespoon baking powder

½ cup whole milk

1 Preheat the oven to 350°F. Grease and flour an 8 x 3-inch round cake pan. Line the bottom of the pan with a round of parchment paper.

2 In a stand mixer with the whisk or paddle attachment, beat the butter, sugar, and eggs on high speed until light and fluffy, about 2 minutes.

3 Using the tip of a sharp knife, scrape the seeds from the vanilla bean into the mixer bowl. (Or add the vanilla extract, if using.) Add the oil to the creamed mixture and combine.

In a small bowl, whisk together the flour and baking powder. Add the flour mixture and milk to the creamed mixture and beat on high speed until the flour is completely mixed, 30 seconds to 1 minute.

5 Scrape the batter into the pan and use an offset spatula to smooth the top.

6 Bake until a wooden skewer inserted into the center of the cake comes out clean, 55 to 60 minutes. Check after 45 minutes, and if the top is browning too much, tent with foil.

7 Cool the cake in the pan for 15 minutes, then run a metal spatula around the edge of the cake and invert onto a wire rack to cool completely.

CLASSIC VANILLA CUPCAKES: Preheat the oven to 350°F. Line 24 cups of muffin tins with paper liners. Make the batter and, using a spoon or ice cream scoop, fill each muffin cup about two-thirds full with batter. Bake until the center of a cupcake springs back when touched, 20 to 22 minutes. Check first at 18 minutes, then each minute thereafter. Cool the cupcakes in the tin for 5 minutes, then remove to a wire rack to cool completely.

CLASSIC CHOCOLATE CAKE & CUPCAKES

Makes two 8 x 2-inch-high cakes or 28 cupcakes

2 sticks (8 ounces) salted butter, at room temperature

1⅔ cups (315g) superfine sugar

1 cup water, at room temperature

3 extra-large eggs, at room temperature

3 tablespoons vegetable oil

2 teaspoons vanilla extract

2¾ cups (340g) all-purpose flour

½ cup plus 2 tablespoons (55g) unsweetened cocoa powder

1 tablespoon baking powder

1 Preheat the oven to 350°F. Grease and flour two 8 x 3-inch round cake pans. Line the bottoms with rounds of parchment paper.

2 In a mixer fitted with the whisk or paddle attachment, beat the butter and sugar until combined. Add the water, eggs, oil, and vanilla and beat on low speed until all ingredients are just combined.

3 In a medium bowl, whisk together the flour, cocoa, and baking powder. Add the flour mixture to the butter mixture and beat on high speed until light and fluffy, 1½ to 2 minutes.

4 Divide the mixture between the two pans and use an offset spatula to smooth the tops.

5 Bake until a skewer inserted into the center of each cake comes out clean, 25 to 30 minutes. Check first at 24 minutes, then each minute thereafter.

CLASSIC CHOCOLATE CUPCAKES: Preheat the oven to 350°F. Line 28 cups of muffin tins with paper liners. Prepare the batter as directed. Using a spoon or ice cream scoop, fill each muffin cup about two-thirds full with batter. Bake until the center of a cupcake springs back when touched, 20 to 22 minutes. Check first at 18 minutes, then each minute thereafter. Cool the cupcakes in the tin for 5 minutes, then remove to a wire rack to cool completely.

WHITE CHOCOLATE MUD CAKE & CUPCAKES

Makes one 9-inch round cake or 28 cupcakes

YOU'LL NEED

2 sticks plus 5 tablespoons (10½ ounces) salted butter

1 cup water

10½ ounces white chocolate, chopped or broken

3⅔ cups (450g) all-purpose flour

2 cups (400g) superfine sugar

3½ teaspoons baking powder

4 extra-large eggs, lightly beaten (room temperature is best)

2 tablespoons plus 1 teaspoon vegetable oil

2 teaspoons vanilla extract (or the seeds from 1 vanilla bean pod)

1 Preheat the oven to 325°F. Grease and flour a 9 x 3-inch round cake pan. Line the bottom with a round of parchment paper.

2 In a saucepan, combine the butter and water over medium heat until they come to a slow boil.

Remove from the heat and add the chocolate, stirring until it's completely melted. Set aside to come to room temperature.

3 In a large bowl, whisk together the flour, sugar, and baking powder and make a well in the center.

4 Pour in the eggs, oil, vanilla, and chocolate mixture and stir vigorously with a wooden spoon until there are no lumps.

5 Pour the batter into the pan, place on a rimmed baking sheet to catch any drips, and bake until a skewer inserted into the center comes out clean, about 1½ hours. If the cake is browning too much on top, cover with some foil about halfway through baking.

6 Allow the cake to completely cool in the pan before removing.

WHITE CHOCOLATE MUD CUPCAKES: Preheat the oven to 350°F. Line 28 cups of muffin tins with paper liners. Prepare the batter as directed. Using a spoon or ice cream scoop, fill each muffin cup about two-thirds full with batter. Bake until the center of a cupcake springs back when touched, 22 to 25 minutes. Check first at 21 minutes, then each minute thereafter. Remove to a wire rack to cool completely.

TIME SAVER: *Mud cakes freeze amazingly well as long as they are double wrapped in plastic. Freeze for up to 1 month.*

RICH CHOCOLATE MUD CAKE & CUPCAKES

Makes one 9-inch round cake or 28 cupcakes

YOU'LL NEED

2 sticks plus 2 tablespoons (9 ounces) salted butter

¾ cup water

2 tablespoons plus 2 teaspoons instant coffee

9 ounces semisweet or milk chocolate, chopped or broken

2⅓ cups all-purpose flour

2⅔ cups (500g) superfine sugar

½ cup plus 3 tablespoons (60g) unsweetened cocoa powder

1½ teaspoons baking powder

1½ teaspoons baking soda

5 extra-large eggs, lightly beaten (room temperature is best)

½ cup buttermilk

5 tablespoons vegetable oil

1 Preheat the oven to 325°F. Grease and flour a 9 x 3-inch round cake pan. Line the bottom with a round of parchment paper.

2 In a saucepan, combine the butter, water, and coffee over medium heat until they come to a slow boil. Remove from the heat and add the chocolate, stirring until it's completely melted. Set aside to cool to room temperature.

3 In a large bowl, whisk together the flour, sugar, cocoa, baking powder, and baking soda and make a well in the center.

4 Pour in the eggs, buttermilk, oil, and chocolate mixture and stir vigorously with a wooden spoon until there are no lumps

5 Pour the batter into the prepared pan and bake until a skewer inserted into the center comes out clean, about 1¼ hours. Allow the cake to completely cool in the pan before removing.

CHOCOLATE MUD CUPCAKES: Preheat the oven to 350°F. Line 28 cups of muffin tins with paper liners. Prepare the batter as directed. Using a spoon or ice cream scoop, fill each muffin cup about two-thirds full with batter. Bake until the center of a cupcake springs back when touched, 24 to 27 minutes. Check first at 23 minutes, then each minute thereafter. Remove to a wire rack to cool completely.

MONEY SAVER: *You can make buttermilk yourself by adding a squeeze of lemon juice to regular whole milk and letting it sit for 10 minutes.*

CHOCOLATE CAKE POP DOUGH

Makes enough for 24 to 36 cake pops

YOU'LL NEED

25 ounces chocolate cake (see Note)

½ cup heavy cream

7 ounces semisweet or milk chocolate, chopped into small pieces

1 Crumble the cake until it resembles fine bread crumbs and place in a bowl.

2 In a microwave-safe bowl, pour the heavy cream over the chocolate. Microwave in 30-second intervals, stirring in between, until the chocolate has completely melted and there are no longer streaks of cream visible.

3 Pour the chocolate mixture over the crumbled cake and stir until well combined. The mixture should hold together like wet sand when squeezed.

4 Store the cake pop dough in zip-seal bags in the freezer for up to 1 month, allowing to come back to room temperature before use.

NOTE: *For reference, one layer of the Classic Chocolate Cake (page 209) weighs about 22 ounces.*

RED VELVET CAKE POP DOUGH

Makes enough for 24 to 36 cake pops

YOU'LL NEED

25 ounces red velvet cake (see box, at right)

½ cup heavy cream

7 ounces white chocolate, chopped into small pieces

Follow the directions for Chocolate Cake Pop Dough (see above).

VANILLA CAKE POP DOUGH

Makes enough for 24 to 36 cake pops

YOU'LL NEED

25 ounces vanilla cake

½ cup heavy cream

7 ounces white chocolate, chopped into small pieces

Follow the directions for Chocolate Cake Pop Dough (at left).

TIME SAVER: *Use a food processor to crumble and mix to save time in the kitchen.*

EASY MICROWAVE CAKE RECIPES

Save some time on baking and get into the decorating part quicker with my simple microwave cake recipes—perfect for cake pop crumbles. This makes just the amount you need for the pop dough.

Microwave Vanilla Cake: In a medium bowl, whisk together ¾ cup plus 1 tablespoon (170g) granulated sugar, 2 cups minus 2 tablespoons (240g) all-purpose flour, and 4 teaspoons baking powder. In another bowl, whisk together ¾ cup hot water, 6 tablespoons plus 2 teaspoons vegetable oil, 1 teaspoon vanilla extract, and 2 extra-large eggs. Pour the liquid mixture over the ingredients and whisk until smooth. Coat the inside of a microwave-safe container (at least 30-ounce capacity) with a generous amount of oil and pour in the mixture. Cover with plastic wrap and microwave on high for 5 minutes (1,000 watts), 7 minutes (800 watts), or 9 minutes (600 watts).

Chocolate Variation: Follow the Vanilla Cake recipe, but omit 6 tablespoons (50g) flour and 1 teaspoon baking powder and replace with ½ cup (45g) unsweetened cocoa powder.

Red Velvet Variation: Replace 1 tablespoon of flour with unsweetened cocoa powder. Add 1 tablespoon red food color paste.

VANILLA SUGAR COOKIES

Makes about 4 dozen 3-inch cookies

YOU'LL NEED

3¼ cups (400g) all-purpose flour, plus more for rolling out the cookies

¼ teaspoon baking soda

¼ teaspoon salt

2 sticks (8 ounces) unsalted butter, at room temperature

¾ cup plus 2 tablespoons (170g) superfine sugar

1 large egg

1 teaspoon vanilla extract

TIP: *Watch your cookies! There's about 1 minute difference between golden brown and burned, so try to stay close while they're baking.*

1 In a large bowl, whisk together the flour, baking soda, and salt.

2 In a stand mixer, beat the butter and sugar until light and fluffy. Add the egg and vanilla and beat until well combined.

3 With the mixer on low, add one-third of the flour mixture and mix to combine. Add the second third of the flour and continue mixing on low speed.

4 Add the final third of the flour mixture, beating just until combined.

5 Pour the mixture onto a work surface and knead with your hands until the dough is no longer crumbly and you are able to form a tight ball, 3 to 5 minutes.

6 Cover the dough in plastic wrap and chill in the fridge for at least 1 hour and preferably 3 hours. You can also leave it in the fridge for up to 3 days or freeze this dough (well wrapped) for up to 1 month.

7 When ready to bake, preheat the oven to 350°F. Line baking sheets with parchment paper.

8 Remove the dough from the fridge and break off a section to work with (I usually use about a third at a time). Give it a quick knead and sprinkle a generous amount of flour on your work surface and also on top of the dough. Using a rolling pin, roll the dough out to a ⅛-inch thickness.

9 Cut out shapes using your desired cookie cutter and place on the baking sheet(s).

10 Bake until the cookies just slightly start to turn golden brown around the edges, 7 to 10 minutes.

11 Immediately transfer the cookies to a cooling rack. Once they are completely cool, decorate as desired.

VANILLA BEAN BUTTERCREAM FROSTING

Makes 4 cups

YOU'LL NEED

2 sticks (8 ounces) unsalted butter, at room temperature
½ vanilla bean (halved crosswise), split lengthwise
5½ cups (650g) powdered sugar
1 to 2 tablespoons whole milk

1 In a stand mixer with the whisk or paddle attachment, beat the butter on high speed for at least 5 minutes, until the butter has lightened in color and is thoroughly whipped.

2 Using the tip of a sharp knife, scrape the vanilla seeds into the butter and beat to incorporate.

3 Add 1 cup of the sugar and begin mixing on low speed to combine, then beat on high speed for about 2 minutes.

4 Repeat this process 1 cup at a time until all the sugar has been added. Add milk a dash at a time if the mixture becomes too thick or dry. Scrape down the sides as needed and make sure no sugar is visible.

5 The frosting will last for 1 month in the freezer, 2 weeks in the fridge, and 3 days at room temperature.

TIP: *This frosting can be tinted using liquid, gel, or paste coloring. You may need to reduce the milk slightly to allow for additional liquid if using liquid colors. Add color after the frosting has been thinned with milk.*

MILK CHOCOLATE
BUTTERCREAM FROSTING

Makes 5 cups

YOU'LL NEED

2 sticks (8 ounces) unsalted butter, at room temperature
1 teaspoon vanilla extract
5½ cups (650g) powdered sugar
5½ tablespoons (30g) unsweetened cocoa powder, sifted
2 to 4 tablespoons whole milk
3½ ounces milk chocolate, melted (see page 220)

1. In a stand mixer with the whisk or paddle attachment, beat the butter on high speed for at least 5 minutes, until the butter has lightened in color and is thoroughly whipped.

2. Beat in the vanilla.

3. Add 1 cup of the sugar and begin mixing on low speed, then beat on high speed for about 2 minutes.

4. Repeat this process 1 cup at a time until all the sugar has been added. Add the cocoa and mix for another 2 minutes.

5. Add milk a dash at a time if the mixture becomes too thick or dry. Scrape down the sides as needed and make sure no sugar is visible.

6. Quickly add the chocolate to the buttercream mixture. Immediately turn the mixer on high and blend the chocolate before it begins to set. Thin to the desired consistency (this will depend on the project) using the remaining milk.

SEVEN-MINUTE FROSTING

Makes 3 cups

YOU'LL NEED

2 large egg whites
1 tablespoon light corn syrup
⅓ cup water
1½ cups (290g) superfine sugar

1 In a large saucepan, bring 3 inches of water to a boil over medium heat, then reduce to a simmer.

2 In a large heatproof bowl, combine the egg whites, corn syrup, water, and sugar. Place the bowl over the pot of simmering water, without the bottom of the bowl touching the water, and with a handheld mixer beat on medium speed until the mixture is thick and fluffy, and soft peaks form, similar to marshmallow creme. Depending on your mixer strength, this could take from 7 to 10 minutes.

> **TIP:** *Turn to this recipe when you need a frosting that is super white. A buttercream can never be "true white" because of the butter (and some people find it a little grainy), so when you're looking for a really white frosting that is ultra smooth and silky, this is for you.*

DARK CHOCOLATE GANACHE

Makes 3 cups

YOU'LL NEED 1¼ cups heavy cream
21 ounces semisweet chocolate, chopped

MICROWAVE METHOD: In a microwave-safe bowl, combine the heavy cream and chocolate and microwave on high in 1-minute intervals, stirring for 2 minutes in between, until there are no lumps. This should take 2 to 3 minutes maximum.

STOVETOP METHOD: In a small saucepan, bring the heavy cream to a rolling boil (this just means a boil with bubbles all over the surface, not just around the outside edges). Remove from the heat and add the chocolate, stirring until there are no lumps.

WORKING WITH GANACHE

- **For pouring and dipping:** Use the ganache while it's still warm. Don't be afraid to dip marshmallows and strawberries into freshly warmed ganache—it's delicious.

- **For whipped, fluffy frosting** (when a piping consistency is needed): Wait until the ganache reaches room temperature, then beat on high speed with an electric mixer until the ganache lightens in color and becomes thick and spoonable.

- **For spreadable consistency** (ideal for layering large cakes, covering cakes, and for use under fondant): Allow the ganache to cool at room temperature for 6 to 8 hours before use. (Try to at least frost your cake before you commence eating the ganache straight from the bowl.)

- **To store:** Cover your ganache with plastic wrap and make sure the wrap touches the surface of the chocolate.

MILK CHOCOLATE GANACHE

Makes 3½ cups

YOU'LL NEED

1¼ cups heavy cream
23 ounces milk chocolate

Follow the directions for Dark Chocolate Ganache (at left).

WHITE CHOCOLATE GANACHE

Makes 3⅓ cups

YOU'LL NEED

1 cup heavy cream
25 ounces white chocolate

Follow the directions for Dark Chocolate Ganache (at left).

TIP: *1 heaped tablespoon of room temperature ganache folded into 1 cup of whipped cream makes an amazing chocolate mousse.*

WORKING WITH CHOCOLATE

First, not all chocolate is the same!

"Real" chocolate contains cocoa butter. If it contains cocoa butter, once you melt it, it will never set up again without "tempering" (a method of stabilizing chocolate). Lots of people melt "real" chocolate and set it in the fridge, where it sets up perfectly well, but when it comes out of the fridge it starts to melt immediately—even in cool climates. It's a guaranteed disaster and a really common problem.

You have three choices:

- Learn how to temper chocolate. I have a great tempering video on the My Cupcake Addiction YouTube channel.
- Use "compound" chocolates, which do not contain cocoa butter.
- Switch to candy melts or melting wafers.

MELTING

Choosing the correct chocolate is only half the battle, and the melting process can be tough. Here are my top tips for perfectly melted, smooth chocolate every time, and achieving the proper consistency to drizzle, pipe, dip, or mold.

Should it be melted in the microwave or on the stovetop?

Both are fine, but a stovetop is a gentler method resulting in fewer instances of burned chocolate. The microwave is quick, easy, and doesn't require multiple containers, but if not done right it can burn your chocolate and result in a gritty, lumpy mess.

STOVETOP METHOD: Place candy melts, coarsely broken-up chocolate, or chocolate chips in a glass or metal bowl. In a small saucepan, bring 2 inches of water to a boil. Remove the pan from the heat and place the bowl on top of the saucepan, making sure the water does not come directly in contact with the bottom of the bowl. Stir occasionally until the chocolate has melted.

MICROWAVE METHOD: Place candy melts, coarsely broken-up chocolate, or chocolate chips in a microwave-safe bowl. Microwave on medium in 30-second intervals, stirring in between, until the chocolate is melted. It may not look like much is happening on the initial stirs, but persist—it generally takes between 2 and 3 minutes to fully melt.

DIPPING, DRIZZLING, OR POURING

For smoother, faster flowing melted chocolate or candy melts, you have two easily available choices to add to the chocolate to thin it to the perfect consistency for dipping, drizzling, or pouring: coconut oil or vegetable shortening.

White chocolate will generally be a great dipping consistency with no additives; dark chocolate is the next best; and milk chocolate will usually need a little help to get smooth and flowing. And for colored candy melts, as well as white candy melts or wafers, I *always* make the mixture a little thinner, because they're tough to work with in the best of times and are very rarely a smooth consistency when melted alone.

The oil or vegetable shortening is added *after* the chocolate has melted so you can judge the consistency of the melted chocolate. As a rule, here are the proportions I go by:

WHITE CHOCOLATE: Nothing needed

DARK CHOCOLATE: 1¼ to 2½ teaspoons vegetable shortening or coconut oil per 3½ ounces

MILK CHOCOLATE: 4 teaspoons vegetable shortening or coconut oil per 3½ ounces

CANDY MELTS: 2 tablespoons vegetable shortening or coconut oil per 3½ ounces

PIPING

If you're piping melted chocolate, it doesn't need to be thinned. If you're using candy melts, however, I would add 4 teaspoons coconut oil or shortening per 3½ ounces of melts to help loosen them up.

White chocolate is generally a little too thin for piping when it's first melted, so I recommend allowing it to sit for 10 minutes so it can thicken up enough to hold its shape.

COLORING

You can add color to melted white chocolate, as well as white candy melts or wafers, using oil- or powder-based food colorings. Liquid-based colorings or any water-based products will cause the chocolate to seize and become a hard, lumpy mess.

> **NOTE**: *Know Your Chocolate!*
> *Compound chocolate does not contain cocoa butter and will reset firm after melting, without needing to be refrigerated. "Real" chocolate contains cocoa butter and requires tempering to be able to stay firm after melting unless kept refrigerated.*

WORKING WITH TIER CAKES & LAYER CAKES

All cakes need some type of preparation, layering, or structure before you can get to the fun part—the decorating!

1 CARVE AND LEVEL

Cakes must be leveled to ensure even layers, soft moist cake layers, and even cake color throughout.

Take the cooled cake and use a serrated knife to carve away a very thin layer from the base of the cake, removing the browned edges **A**.

Using a bread knife and a steady hand (or a cake leveler for a precise result), slice the top of the cake flat **B**. For multilayered cakes, make sure all the cake layers are of even height.

2 STACK AND LAYER

Split the cake horizontally into the desired number of layers, cutting across evenly **C**. Getting down to eye level with your cake helps keep your line straight.

Place a small amount of frosting onto a cake board or plate to hold your cake in place. Lay the first layer of cake on top of the frosting in the center of the board. Sometimes the layer will be brushed with a simple syrup until it is just moistened. The simple syrup adds moisture and can extend the life of your cake by a few extra days.

Place a small amount of frosting onto the cake and use an offset spatula to spread the frosting in a back-and-forth motion to create a very thin layer that will catch any stray crumbs **D**. Then apply a generous amount of frosting and spread it across the cake layer, letting the frosting protrude slightly over the edges of the cake layers.

Repeat the stacking and layering for all the remaining layers.

3 ADD SUPPORTS (FOR TALL CAKES)

If your cake contains fewer than five 1-inch layers of cake, there is no need to add central support. But if your cake has 5 layers or more, you will need to add support to the bottom layers so the upper layers don't cause the cake to collapse. A central cake board is also added to make the cake easier to serve.

To add support, I use either fat straws (which are easy to cut) or dowels (a little harder to cut). I use 4 supports in a 6-inch-diameter cake, 6 supports in an 8-inch cake, and 8 supports in a 10-inch cake.

The supports will be added when you have assembled half the layers (so, for example, after the fourth layer for an 8-layer cake, or after the fifth layer for a 10-layer cake). Start by stacking and layering the bottom half of the cake. Then place a support into the center of the cake, pushing down until it hits the cake board. Cut the supports so they are in line with the top of the cake **E**. Scissors are fine for straws and pruning shears work well for dowels.

Add the supports spaced evenly in a circle around the center of the cake, making sure that if your upper tiers are smaller than the tier below the supports will fit within the diameter of the cake above.

Place a cake board 1 inch smaller in diameter than your upper cake layers on top of the supports **F**, add a small amount of frosting, and start layering and frosting the upper layer of cake.

4 FROST AND SMOOTH

Once your cake is leveled, layered, and, if necessary, supported, it's time to frost the outside of the cake. Take a small amount of frosting and use an offset spatula to apply a very thin coat of frosting to the outside walls and top of your cake, firmly working the spatula back and forth and allowing the frosting to fill in any gaps between the layers and catch any stray crumbs **G**. This is called the "crumb coat."

Refrigerate 20 minutes to set the crumb coat.

Once set, apply a generous amount of frosting—more than you think you'll need—and distribute it evenly around the sides and on the top.

Hold a ruler or scraper up against the side of the cake **H** and drag it around the outside of the cake, allowing the frosting to be scraped back to a smooth, flat, seamless surface—wipe your ruler or scraper to remove excess frosting, then repeat, making sure you don't press too firmly and expose the cake beneath.

Once the sides are smooth and even, use the ruler or scraper like a cement leveler and drag it across the top of the cake for a smooth, flat, even finish. Aim to keep the edges of your cake sharp and precise.

5 SERVE

Slide a cake server or cake lifter under the bottom cake board **I** and move the cake carefully to your presentation plate, stand, or platter. Doing this now allows for any mishaps that may occur before the final decorating is done. Serving a tiered cake **J** is a lot easier when the cake has supports, and you get more servings: Instead of trying to cut a huge, tall piece of cake, simply cut the top cake as normal, stopping at the center cake board. Once the entire top cake has been served, remove the center cake board and base supports and serve the bottom cake as normal.

TEMPLATES

PICKET FENCE, PAGE 78

"MAKE A SPLASH"
DRIP CAKE, PAGE 86

MOSAIC HEART CAKE,
PAGE 38

COOKIE BUNTING FLAG,
PAGE 22

TEMPLATES

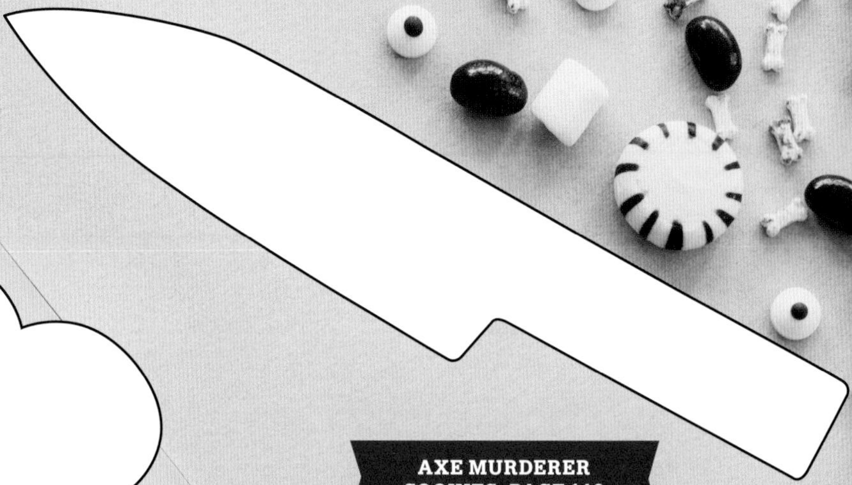

AXE MURDERER
COOKIES, PAGE 140

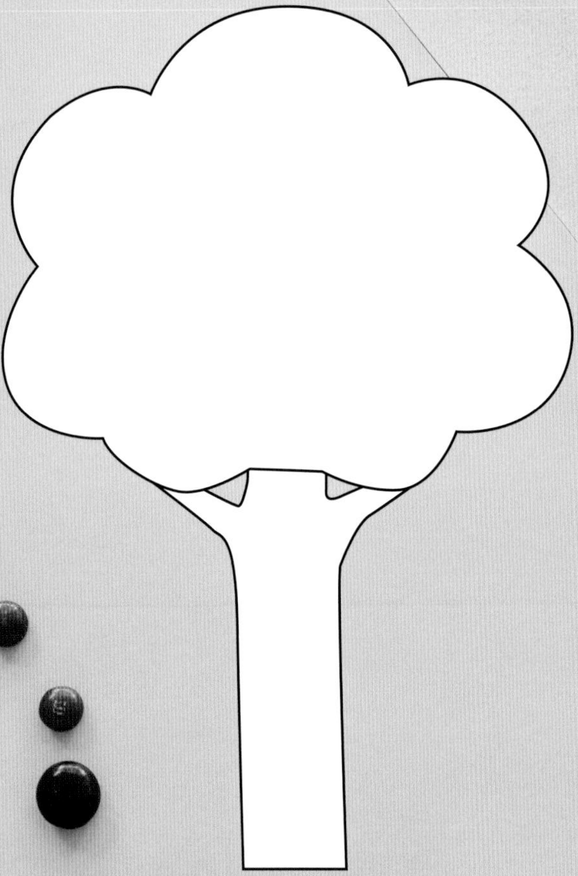

UNDER THE APPLE
TREE LAYERED CAKES,
PAGE 166

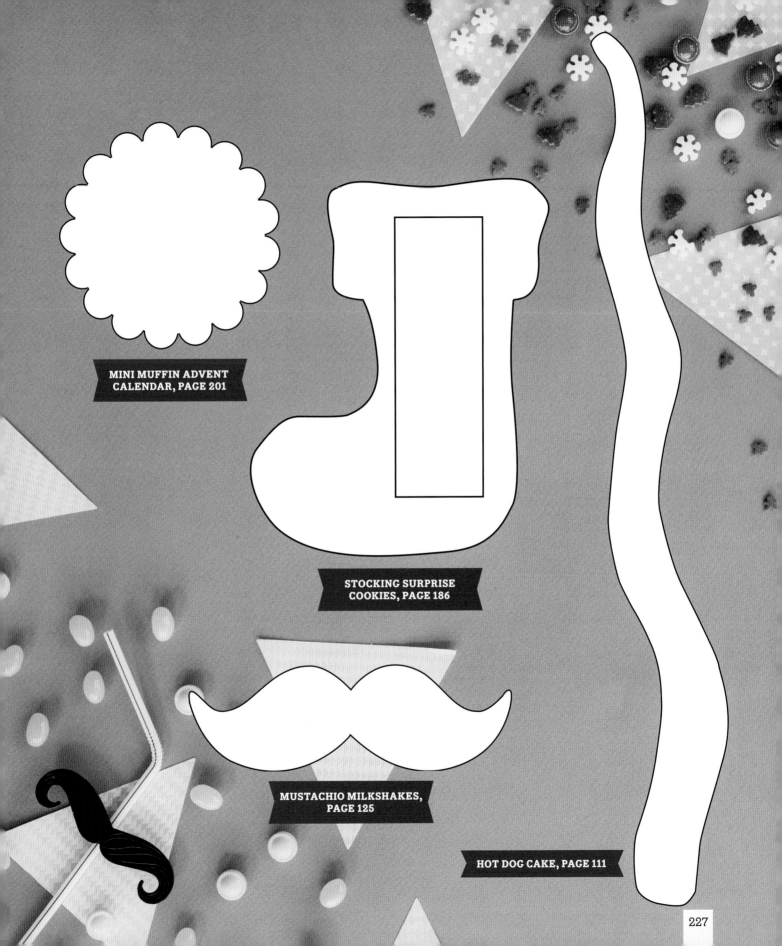

MINI MUFFIN ADVENT
CALENDAR, PAGE 201

STOCKING SURPRISE
COOKIES, PAGE 186

MUSTACHIO MILKSHAKES,
PAGE 125

HOT DOG CAKE, PAGE 111

INDEX

ACKNOWLEDGMENTS

Bringing this book to life truly took a "village." No fewer than twenty people were involved in the creation of this beautiful publication, and I could not have done this without each and every one of you.

TO MY PUBLISHER, JUDITH, AND EDITOR, JOHANNA: Thank you for seeing my vision and allowing me to run with it.

TO KATE AND SANDY IN NEW YORK: Thank you for your hard work and advice throughout the production of the book.

TO MY MANAGER, LISA GOLDSTONE (below): When we decided to write a book, it signaled the start of months and months of late nights, tight deadlines, and huge learning curves—not to mention all the cakes we had to test!

Thank you for your hard work, professionalism, amazing organizational skills, and sunny nature throughout this project.

Without you, this book would still be light-years away—you're truly one in a million.

TO MY AMAZING PHOTOGRAPHY AND STYLING TEAM: Each of the hands in this picture worked tirelessly to shoot the images and help me re-create the crazy recipes inside this book.

LAUREN BAMFORD: Photographer

STEPHANIE STAMATIS: Stylist

CAROLINE VELIK: Food styling

CAITLIN BELL: Home economist

AND TO THE UNSUNG HEROES: The numerous assistants who climbed trees, spray painted accessories, and helped to make this book possible, thank you Merril, Ella, Emily, Larissa, and Emma.

TO CANDICE AND SARAH: Thank you for being my glam squad!